New England Meeting House and Church: 1630-1850

A Loan Exhibition held at The Currier Gallery of Art, Manchester, New Hampshire

Peter Benes & Philip D. Zimmerman

Published by Boston University and The Currier Gallery of Art for The Dublin Seminar for New England Folklife

This catalogue and the exhibition it accompanies have been made possible through the generous support of the National Endowment for the Humanities, Washington, D.C., a Federal agency.

Copies are available by mail from: Boston University Scholarly Publications, 25 Buick St., Boston, MA 02215. Price: $7.95 each, plus $.50 postage and handling charge per copy.

Dates of the exhibition: May 19–July 15, 1979

The Currier Gallery of Art, Manchester, New Hampshire

Copyright © 1979 by the Trustees of Boston University, and by The Currier Gallery of Art

Library of Congress Catalog Card Number 79–53115

ISBN 0–87270–050–X

Designed by Richard Hendel

The Dublin Seminar for New England Folklife is a continuing series of conferences and exhibitions designed to explore the daily life, work, and culture of the common man in New England's past. Sponsored jointly by the Dublin School and by Boston University's American and New England Studies Program, the series focuses attention on emerging areas of folk studies, regional and local history, cultural geography, social history, historical archeology, vernacular arts, material culture, and antiquarian studies. The Dublin Seminar for New England Folklife was chartered as a nonprofit corporation in the State of New Hampshire in 1978. Address enquiries to the Director, The Dublin Seminar for New England Folklife, Dublin, New Hampshire 03444.

Foreword

This catalogue commemorates the first comprehensive exhibition on the subject of the New England Meeting House and Church. The exhibition was designed to present not only the architectural features of these structures but the artifacts traditionally found within them, and to lead the viewer to consider both architecture and artifacts within the context of their place and time. In selecting the objects for display, attention was given to their spiritual function, as well as to their aesthetic value and antiquarian interest, and we trust that the viewer will perceive the unusual transformation that occasionally occurs from their mutual association.

An exhibition and catalogue of this scope represents the collaborative efforts of a number of dedicated people. We are especially grateful to Peter Benes and Philip Zimmerman of the Dublin Seminar for New England Folklife. Benes originally conceived the concept, Zimmerman helped enlarge it, and together they organized every detail with tact, intelligence and taste. And, of course, we are deeply grateful to those institutions and individuals who generously parted with their possessions for the duration of the show: without the kindly cooperation of these lenders, the exhibition would clearly have been impossible. We also wish to thank Daniel Farber for supplying many of the photographs for this catalogue, Richard Hendel of *The Word Guild* of Cambridge for designing it, and Pat Mahon of Boston University for guiding it through production. The exhibition and catalogue were financed by a grant from the National Endowment for the Humanities, and we wish to express our gratitude to its staff for their helpful guidance and advice.

Robert M. Doty, Director
The Currier Gallery of Art

Patrick Gregory, Editor
Boston University Scholarly Publications

Contents

Preface

New England Meeting House and Church: 1630–1850 was originally conceived as the topic for the fourth meeting of the Dublin Seminar for New England Folklife (held 23 and 24 June 1979), an annual series of conferences and exhibitions exploring the daily life, work, and culture of the common man in New England's past. The exhibition was designed around the underlying philosophy and strength of the Dublin Seminar, which lies in broad participation by interested amateurs and professionals. To this end local historical societies, museums, libraries, churches, and private individuals, in addition to the well-known large museums and societies in New England, were approached as sources for artifacts, information, and ideas. The responses to these inquiries were generous, and they have played a key role in the selection of the exhibited material and in its description and interpretation in the catalogue.

As described in our search letter, the purpose of the exhibition was to re-create in its entirety the "world" of the early New England meeting house and church. This "world" includes not only social, political, and religious functions but also the musical and artistic expressions that took place or were embodied within the meeting house and church. Since so much of what is known about New England meeting houses has come down through oral tradition, our aim was to challenge or corroborate this knowledge with artifactual evidence, architectural fragments, and documentary data; to put its folklore, myth, and nostalgic elements into a historical perspective; and to refine or redraw this picture as the evidence might reasonably suggest.

As the search for artifacts and objects progressed, the evidence that came to light increasingly revealed the ambiguity and complexity of the meeting house and the traditions and practices that were associated with it. Low rates of survival and incomplete or conflicting data were major obstacles to our understanding. The ambiguity of the written record made accurate interpretations difficult. Perhaps the greatest challenge, however, came in trying to separate fact from legend. At the center of the world of the meeting house is a delicate structure of folklore—born out of historical circumstances but colored by layers of embellishment as stories and information were passed from generation to generation. These stories, which fortunately have been preserved in many nineteenth-century town histories, often provide the background and the specific details necessary to grasp the meaning of many facets of the meeting house. At the same time, they have occasionally been the source of misconceptions and misinterpretations. Some traditions could, of course, be readily identified as myths. The eighteenth-century claim that the only way to put out a steeple fire was by dousing it with pails of milk is just that—a story based on folklore and legend that might be traced to English parish lore. But how accurate is the "feather and ball" tithing stick tradition? Or the secondhand recollections that cherub faces were sometimes painted on either side of early nineteenth-century pulpits?

What remained was a world of considerable variety within what appeared to be a set of common New England forms. Our task was to sketch these forms where we could accurately and clearly perceive them and to identify those areas where conflicting evidence or a lack of data made this impossible. To facilitate the organization and presentation of the exhibited material in the short time that was available, our inquiry focused on Congregational meeting houses and churches. Treatment of related denominations of Baptists, Presbyterians, and Anglicans was restricted to providing a clearer idea of Congregational practice. Other sects, like Quakers, Moravians, Sandemanians, and Shakers had to be eliminated entirely. Similarly, the time span was selected so that we could concentrate on seventeenth- and eighteenth-century conditions, yet carry many of these ideas through to their resolution in the first half of the nineteenth century.

It was also necessary to limit the thematic scope of our inquiry. The principal question addressed in our search was the relationship between ecclesiastical and civic forms. What began as a common domestic form—be it a "long" house, a chalice, a wooden tankard, or an earthenware jug—set in motion a chain of events that resulted in the definition of an ecclesiastical form. Were these forms related to English ecclesiastical usage? At what point did ecclesiastical forms define themselves independently from their secular origin? More important, once these forms were defined, did they easily assume the veneer of contemporary secular modes and ornamentation?

Here again considerable ambiguity entered into our efforts. The only church- or meetinghouse-related objects that have survived in large enough numbers to provide a reliable data base are communion silver vessels, whose provenances are generally known regardless of who now owns them. Moreover, they are usually marked and are often cited in church records. Other objects, such as tithing sticks, spitboxes, and furniture, have experienced high attrition or have lost their meetinghouse associations, so that it is difficult or impossible to reconstruct evolutionary sequences in style and form or to chart their geographical or chronological distribution.

What is said of certain historical epochs may be true, too, of the subject we have tried to explore. If the world of the New England meeting house did not exist as tradition now remembers it, later generations may have had to invent this world. Nevertheless, if our reconstruction of the early New England meeting house and church has been enhanced by a greater measure of truth, the search and exhibition will have met their objectives.

The Meeting House

Meeting house as a term first occurs in American usage in 1632, when John Winthrop alludes in his *Journal* to the "new meeting house" at Dorchester, Massachusetts. By it he meant, simply, the house that had recently been built in Dorchester for the purpose of holding religious and secular meetings. The term was deeply significant because implied in its use was a definition of the term *church* that distinguished the Puritans who accompanied Winthrop from the members of the Church of England whom they left behind. To Winthrop, a church was a covenanted body of people. As Richard Mather was to state later, "There is no just ground in Scripture to apply such a trope as church to a house for public assembly."[1]

To its builders, therefore, the meeting house was an architectural expression of the Reformed point of view that the "house of God" was not a sacred place. At the same time, it represented an expedient, if temporary, joining of a number of secular buildings: powder house, court house, school house, meeting hall, town house, parsonage, and fort. And while its final termination coincided with the legal separation of church and state in New England in the early nineteenth century, the actual demise of the meeting house came gradually, as each of its secular functions assumed an independent form.

In current usage, the term *meeting house* has developed both a narrow and a broad definition. Architectural historians distinguish a meeting-house plan from a church plan by the so-called short-side alignment of the main entry and pulpit. In a meeting house, the pulpit and entryway face each other across the narrow dimension of the building; in a church, the principal entry and pulpit face each other across its length. To a social historian, however, a meeting house is a combined municipal and religious structure erected and supported by public taxation regardless of its architectural details.

Combining these definitions, a meeting house can be seen as any ecclesiastical structure built by public taxation regardless of its floor plan and any structure built by a private society in which the pulpit-entry axis is on the short side. This definition includes the 1817 Fitzwilliam, New Hampshire, meeting house, which was designed on a church plan but which was a public structure serving both municipal and ecclesiastical purposes. But it excludes almost all Anglican churches in New England except for one or two early examples, such

1. John Winthrop, *Winthrop's Journal: A History of New England 1630–1649*, ed. James K. Hosmer, 2 vols. (1908; reprint ed., Barnes & Noble, 1966), 1:75; J. Frederick Kelly, *Early Connecticut Meetinghouses*, 2 vols. (New York: Columbia University Press, 1948), p. xxiv.

as St. Paul's at Wickford, Rhode Island, built in 1707. It also excludes structures like the 1772 Brattle Square Church in Boston, the 1772 North Church in Salem, Massachusetts, and the 1775 First Baptist Church in Providence, Rhode Island, all of which were erected by private subscription following a church plan. Under this definition, the only meeting houses built after the legal separation of church and state in New England were those constructed by Quaker societies.

The New England Parish System

Historical accounts indicate that the annual number of meeting houses and churches built from 1630 to 1850 varied anywhere between none and thirty with a yearly average of about fifteen to twenty. This average indicates that between three and four thousand such structures were raised in New England during this period, a figure that can be broken down by century: approximately two hundred and twenty meeting houses were built in the seventeenth century; approximately two thousand (plus a handful of churches) in the eighteenth century; and another thousand in the first half of the nineteenth century, about half of these churches.

These numbers represent a demographic reality that goes to the heart of the role meeting houses played in early New England history. The number of meeting houses erected in a given town depended on the quantity and distribution of its population and its ecclesiastical unity. Every town had at least one meeting house at an early point in its history. Indeed, one of the principal requirements a town's proprietors had to fulfill before receiving title from the colonial authorities, besides having to attract a minimum number of settlers, was to hire a minister and erect a meeting house within a specified number of years. Thereafter, additional meeting houses were determined by the creation of demographic subdivisions within the town. Termed *precincts* or *parishes* (in Connecticut precincts were usually called *societies*), each was legally required to have its own meeting house, minister, and schoolteacher. In addition, most parishes set aside a public burying ground. For example, when the Second Society in Kennebunk, Maine, was formed in 1750, a warrant was written and posted by the parish clerk calling the new society together for its first meeting. The new Second Society incorporated itself under the laws of the Province of Massachusetts without opposition from the First Society. But this was not always the case. Precinct divisions were often hotly contested by the residents of the older precinct, whose tax rates would increase as a result of such a move. Once a new precinct won legal recognition from the colonial General Court, it was no longer required to pay for the minister and meeting house of the old precinct.

Whether accomplished legally or extralegally, the creation of a new precinct redistributed the financial and administrative base of a town's religious, educational, and civic responsibilities in such a way that these activities generally remained on a community scale. The costs of erecting a meeting house and hiring a minister made it impossible to generate a precinct of under thirty or forty families. By the same token, the precinct base was not likely to exceed two hundred families because of the inherently limited seating capacities of frame-built meeting houses, which on the average were able to accommodate no more than six hundred people.

As a result, the majority of New Englanders before 1850 lived in what amounted to communities of fifty to one hundred families. These may or may not have matched town boundaries as they are known today and in some instances may have been defined denominationally or factionally. Each community unit was responsible for the management of its own religious, educational, and civic life. At the center of each was the meeting house, with its principal entry facing south and its pulpit attached to the opposite (north) wall. The meeting house served as a place to hold weekly religious and secular gatherings. It also served as a focus of important public events. Here were held singing concerts and the annual town meeting. Here were celebrated the baptisms, weddings, and funerals that marked the beginning, midpoint, and end of the life of every individual in the community.

Seventeenth-Century Meeting Houses

The first meeting places in New England were large dwelling houses. John Winthrop's parlor or chamber served this purpose in Boston in 1630, as did a "Great House" in Charlestown in 1635.[2] A variant of this form was the combined parsonage and meeting house, or parsonage and chapel, such as was built in Portsmouth, New Hampshire, in 1640. Defensive structures were also an early form. The 1657 contract of the second meeting house in Portsmouth, New Hampshire, describes what in effect was a 40-foot square blockhouse whose sides were "to be of Loggs 9 Inches thick." If oral tradition is reliable (it is partially substantiated by archaeological and architectural data), the

2. Marian C. Donnelly, *The New England Meeting Houses of the Seventeenth Century* (Middletown, Conn.: Wesleyan University Press, 1968), p. 10; Richard Frothingham, *The History of Charlestown, Massachusetts* (Boston: Little, Brown, 1845), p. 95.

3. George M. Adams, *An Historical Discourse Delivered at the Celebration of the Two-Hundredth Anniversary of the Formation of the North Church, Portsmouth, N.H.* (Portsmouth, N.H.: Robinson, 1871), p. 25; Beverly Anderson, Sarah Langley, and Abbie Morasky-Smith, "Archeological Investigations at the Grounds of the Henry Whitfield State Historical Museum in Guilford, Connecticut," *Annual Proceedings of the Dublin Seminar for New England Folklife* (1977): *New England Historical Archeology*, 36–43.

4. *The Ancient Records of Norwalk, Connecticut*, ed. Edwin Hall (Norwalk, Conn.: J. Mallory & Co., 1847), p. 49; James Deetz, *In Small Things Forgotten: The Archeology of Early American Life* (Garden City, N.Y.: Anchor Press, Doubleday, 1977), pp. 98–99, 102.

5. J. Rupert Simonds, *History of the First Church and Society of Branford, Connecticut* (New Haven: Tuttle, Morehouse, 1919), p. 48; Sylvester Judd, *History of Hadley, Massachusetts* (Northampton, Mass.: Metcalf, 1836), p. 42; F. M. Caulkins, *History of Norwich, Connecticut: 1660–1845* (Norwich, Conn.: Thomas Robinson, 1845), p. 126.

stone house built by the Reverend Henry Whitfield in Guilford, Connecticut (1639), not only served as the meeting house of his small congregation but as a defensive fort as well.[3]

In the absence of a definite architectural tradition transplanted to New England, meeting houses during the later period of settlement (1640–1690) assumed what appears to have been a variety of architectural types, none of which was necessarily dominant at any time. One of these was the posthole meeting house, known from a description in the 1659 contract for a meeting house in Norwalk, Connecticut, which was "to be set upon posts in the ground, 12 foot in length, that there be a 10 foot distance from the ground to the ————." Because of the fragmentary and ambiguous nature of the document, it is not known whether the Norwalk structure was elevated off the ground like seventeenth-century English market halls or whether its sills were mortised in at ground level. In either case, vertical posts set into the ground provided the foundation for the building instead of the more common underpinning of stone. Seventeenth-century domestic parallels of posthole meeting houses have been found in the Plymouth Colony and possibly in Guilford, Connecticut.[4]

Another meetinghouse form that had a domestic parallel was the "long house," so-called after the "long brick house with a leanto" referred to in the Branford, Connecticut, records of 1699. Long houses are known to have been constructed in Hadley, Massachusetts (1663), and Norwich, Connecticut (1673); both of these long houses were enlarged by lean-tos. The 1639 meeting house in Marblehead, Massachusetts, was similarly enlarged.[5] Judging by dimensions such as the 40- by 22-foot meeting house in Hampton, New Hampshire (1640), and the 45- by 25-foot meeting house in Springfield, Massachusetts (1645), the long house was a widely used form.

By the end of the seventeenth century, the meeting house had acquired a dominant form. It consisted of a square or nearly square plan, provisions for one or two galleries, a hipped roof, and up to four large gables, usually with windows. Some of these houses were sizable—for example, the 50-foot square buildings at New Haven (1640), Wethersfield (1686), Hartford (1638), and Stamford (1640), Connecticut. More often, they were erected with 30- or 40-foot dimensions. The 55- by 45-foot hipped-roof meeting house (1681) in Hingham, Massachusetts, now known as "Old Ship" from the curvature of its truss rafters, is the only remaining example of this form of architecture, though additions and changes have altered its seventeenth-century form. A surviving casement window from this meeting house reveals

57. Two casement windows from the "Old Ship" meeting house in Hingham, Mass., 1681.

the diamond-shaped quarrel panes that were then in use (Figure 57).*

A more accurate conception of the exterior appearance of this type can be gained from an illustration of the second meeting house in New Haven, Connecticut (1669), which is shown on the Wadsworth map of 1748 (Figure 37). Drawn while this structure was still standing, the map was issued in a printed format with some modifications in 1806.[6] An illustration of the hipped-roof 1694 meeting house in Deerfield, Massachusetts, was drawn in the eighteenth century by Dudley Woodbridge in the pages of his diary, together with what may have been representations of similar but larger buildings in West Springfield and other towns in the Connecticut River Valley (Figure 10).

Additional details concerning square meeting houses can be inferred from the language of the contract concluded in 1658 between the selectmen of Malden, Massachusetts, and the carpenter Job Lane for the building of a "good strong, Artificial meeting house . . . of Thirty-three foot square, sixteen foot stud between joints, with dores, windows, pullpit, seats." The initial clauses in this contract provide

    1. That all the sells, girts, mayne posts, plates, Beames and all

6. The 1806 printed version of this map indicates that it is derived from a 1748 manuscript map by "Gen. Wadsworth of Durham." This was probably James Wadsworth, born in Durham, Connecticut, in 1730; he graduated from Yale in 1748 and served as a brigadier general in the Connecticut militia during the Revolution. See *Appleton's Cyclopedia of American Biography*, 6 vols. (N.Y.: D. Appleton, 1889), 6:312.

* The figure numbers in this essay correspond to the catalogue numbers in the back of the book.

37. New Haven, Conn., as it appeared in 1748.

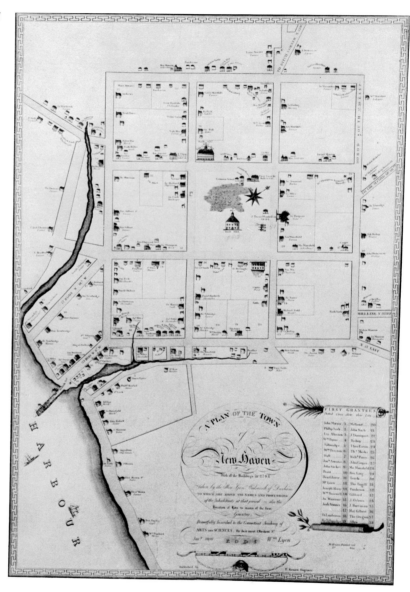

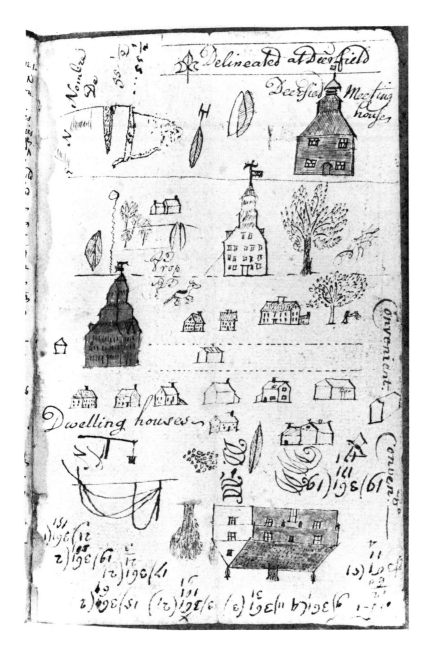

10. *The second meeting house in Deerfield, Mass., as it appeared in October 1728.*

7. *Bicentennial Book of Malden* (Boston: Rand, 1850), p. 124; Myron O. Allen. *History of Wenham* (Boston: Bazin & Chandler, 1860), p. 195.

other principal Timbers shall be of good and sound white or Black oake.

2. That all the walls be made upp on the outside with good clapboards, well dressed lapped and nayled. And the Inside to be lathed all over and well struck with clay, and uppon it with lime and hard up to the wall plate, and also the beame fellings as need shalbe.

3. The roofe to be covered with boards and short shinglings with a territt on the topp about six foot squar, to hang the bell in with rayles about it: the floor to be made tite with planks.

5. Thre dores in such places as the syd Selectment shal direct, viz: east, west and south.

6. Six windows below the girt on thre sids . . . to contayne sixteen foot of glass in a window, with Leaves, and two windows on the south side above the girt on each side of the deske, to contayne six foot of glass. . . .

No weather vane is mentioned in the Malden contract. However, the iron flag erected in 1688 on the second meeting house in Wenham, Massachusetts (1663), is representative of similar seventeenth-century meetinghouse vanes, and one like it probably was placed on the "territ" of the Malden structure (Figure 51).[7]

Perhaps the best-known example of the square meeting house is the 72- by 54-foot "Old Brick" in Boston, constructed by the First Boston Church shortly after its second meeting house was consumed by the fire of 1711. Furnished with a front stairwell porch and clock, the two-gallery Old Brick was the largest and one of the last hipped-roof meeting houses in New England. A nineteenth-century lithograph shows it with a pilastered two-story stairwell porch, which replaced the original porch in 1784 (Figure 15).

Eighteenth-Century Meeting Houses

Early in the eighteenth century, the roofs of meeting houses changed from a hipped design with gable inset windows to a gable-ended design. The records call these by several terms. A "flattish roof" was built in Hadley, Massachusetts (1713), a "long roof" in Bridgeport, Connecticut (1716), a "straight roof" in East Haven, Connecticut

51. Flag weather vane from the second meeting house in Wenham, Mass., 1688.

8

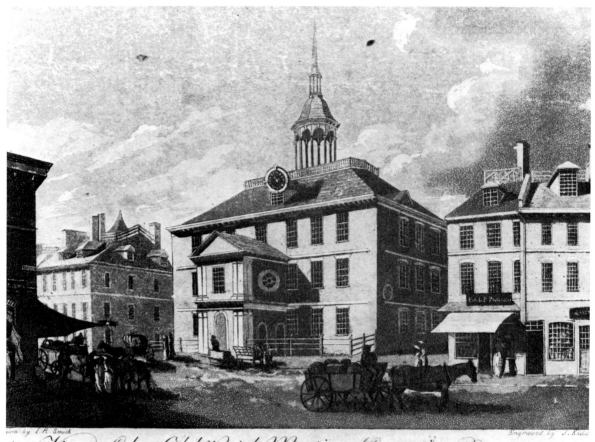

View of the Old Brick Meeting House in Boston 1808.

15. 1808 view of Old Brick meeting house in Boston, Mass.

(1717), a roof built in "barn fation" in Westfield, Massachusetts (1720). An example of this new roof design is found on the 1712 meeting house in Lexington, Massachusetts, a double-gallery structure shown in the background of Amos Doolittle's line engraving, *The Battle of Lexington, 1775* (Figure 20). The Lexington meeting house was provided with an external standing belfry. However, judging by the numbers of "bell coneys" (belfries) and platforms that were still being erected on them, the new roof designs were not a radical departure from the seventeenth-century "square" meeting house, and some communities simply changed roofs in order to keep up with the new styles. The

The Battle of Lexington. April 19th 1775. Plate 1.

20. The Battle of Lexington, 1775.

pen drawing of the 1683 meeting house in Plymouth, Massachusetts, shown with quarrel window glass and a belfry in the center of the roof, illustrates a presumed conversion from a hipped four-gable to a "long" roof design in the eighteenth century (Figure 9a). The smaller and less exact sketch of a four-gable structure to the upper right of this drawing may be a representation of the 1683 meeting house as it was originally built. A comparable conversion was made by Newbury, Massachusetts, when it voted in 1726 "that the four Gable ends in ye Roof of ye meeting House be Taken Down and that each Part opened thereby be well timbered and boarded and shingled."[8]

8. Judd, *History of Hadley*, p. 318; Samuel Orcutt, *A History of the Old Town of Stratford and the City of Bridgeport, Connecticut* (New Haven: Fairfield Co. Historical Society, 1886), pp. 480–482; D. William Havens, *Historical Discourse, Centennial Celebration of the Stone Meeting House in East Haven* (New Haven: Punderson & Crisand, 1876), p. 19; *History of the Connecticut Valley in Massachusetts,*

11

9a. Two views of the second meeting house in Plymouth, Mass., built 1683.

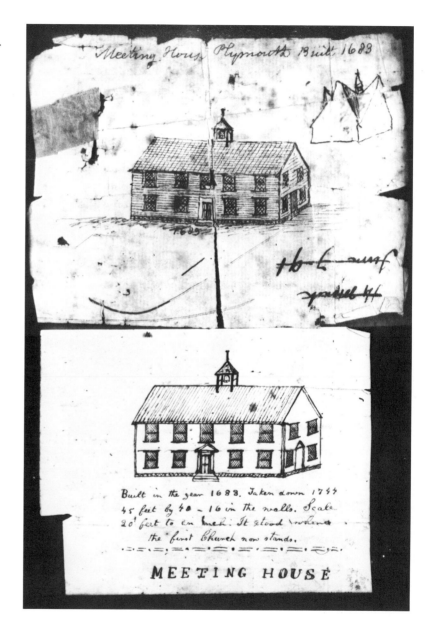

MEETING HOUSE

The shift to long roofs encountered at least some resistance. East Windsor, Connecticut, which voted to raise a new 40-foot square meeting house in 1710, specified at the time they were actually building the structure, in 1713, that the "roof of the new meeting house shall be as this is." This vote, presumably taken in their first meeting house, erected about 1695 with the hipped-type roof, directed the builders to construct the new roof in the old way.[9]

The Church of England, in the meantime, was establishing a distinct architectural form, within both New England and the American colonies as a whole, which was largely based on English antecedents. With the building of the first King's Chapel in Boston (1688), St. Paul's in Narragansett, Rhode Island (1707), St. Michael's in Marblehead, Massachusetts (1714), Christ Church in Boston (1723), and the second Trinity Church in Newport (1726), a conventional Anglican form emerged whose constituent elements, like an unspoken but highly visible code, distinguished its houses of worship from multifunctional Puritan meeting houses. The three principal elements of this code were a standing bell tower and spire, a church plan, and "compass" or round-topped windows. The nineteenth-century lithograph of Trinity Church in Newport, with its second bell tower, built in 1762 (the first was blown down in a gale in 1731), illustrates all three elements (Figure 18). Appropriately, they are also found on the church in the background of the mourning picture by Hannah Punderson of Preston, Connecticut, whose family belonged to the Episcopal church in that town (Figure 47).

Within the church, too, Anglican builders developed distinctive decorative modes not common to the Puritan tradition. The winged cherub head from Trinity Church in Boston, a rare surviving example of eighteenth-century New England ecclesiastical painting, was one of several similar representations painted by John Gibbs on canvas and probably located in the chancel or apse (Figure 124). It may have resembled the "6 Cherubims heads with fustoons of Musick" known to have been painted in Christ Church in Boston and subsequently painted over.[10]

At times, builders of Anglican houses of worship simulated their distinguishing "codes." The *trompe l'oeil* window panel recently recovered by restoration architects from St. Michael's in Marblehead is one of two round-topped window caps painted on wooden panels that were placed over each of the squared windows of the building, thus giving the appearance of Anglican-styled rounded windows (Figure 58). A close inspection of this panel reveals that square or sash lights

2 vols. (Philadelphia: L. H. Everts, 1879), 2:947; John James Currier, *History of Newbury, Mass. 1635–1902* (Boston: Damrell, 1902), p. 337.

9. Henry R. Stiles, *History of Ancient Windsor, Connecticut*, 2 vols. (New York: C. B. Norton, 1859), 1:151.

10. Mary Babcock, *Christ Church, Boston* (Boston: Todd, 1947), p. 244.

18. Trinity Church, Newport, R.I., erected 1726.

47. Mourning picture by Hannah Punderson, Preston, Conn., ca. 1820–1825.

124. Fragment from an interior painting in Trinity Church, Boston, Mass., ca. 1755.

58. Rounded window cap from St. Michael's Church, Marblehead, 1714.

were overpainted on an earlier set of diamond quarrels sometime after the latter went out of fashion early in the eighteenth century.

While a pure Anglican architectural form can be theorized, the inconsistency of its application reinforces the view that Puritan and Anglican forms were opposite extremes in the larger spectrum of the same Reformed tradition. St. Paul's in Wickford, Rhode Island (1707), used rounded windows but followed a meetinghouse plan: The pulpit faced the main entry across the narrow dimension. When the building was moved from its original site in Narragansett, Rhode Island, to Wickford in 1799, its interior was "turned" in order to conform to a church plan.[11] This plan and a steeple added at a later date are incorporated in a model of this church made in the late nineteenth century (Figure 68). A woodcut of the 1737 Trinity Church in Boston illustrates that this building was also outside the conventional idiom of Anglican architecture (Figure 19).

However imprecisely they were defined in the colonial context, the existence of Anglican "codes" provided an innovative architectural standard that few New Englanders were able to resist. Throughout the eighteenth century, meeting house builders either adopted or at least simulated important aspects of the Anglican forms that these structures exhibited. Some congregations gravitated toward these forms more readily than others. The Brattle Square Church in Boston is an extreme case in a gradation of "high" or Anglican-inclined Congregational societies that adopted the codes that marked the general style of the Church of England. At its founding in 1699, this society agreed to read Scripture from the pulpit, to discontinue the practice of "lining out" the Psalms, and to make the public "relation" of the conversion experience optional. It was one of the first "dissenting" societies in New England to build a standing bell tower. In 1772 it built its second meeting house along a church plan, the first non-

11. Harold Wickliffe Rose, *The Colonial Houses of Worship in America* (New York: Hastings House, 1963), p. 408.

19. 1834 woodcut of Trinity Church, Boston, Mass., erected 1734.

15

*68. Model of St. Paul's Church, 1707,
Narragansett, R.I.*

12. *Records of the Church in Brattle
    Square 1699–1872* (Boston: Benev-
    olent Fraternity, 1902), p. 5;
    Samuel K. Lothrop, *A History of
    the Church in Brattle Street, Boston*
    (Boston: Crosby & Nichols,
    1851), p. 46.
13. Judd, *History of Hadley*, p. 318.

Anglican congregation to do this. Each of these decisions brought the Brattle society a step closer to formal Anglican practice.[12]

The shift in the early eighteenth century from hipped to "flattish" or "long" roofs allowed builders to mimic or simulate Anglican "steeple houses" by placing the bell coney at one of the gable ends of the roof rather than in the center. When Hadley, Massachusetts, for example, built its 50- by 40-foot second meeting house in 1713, the town specified a "flattish roof and a balcony at one end" (an arrangement that was impossible with a hipped roof).[13] The structure resembled the Anglican building with its standing bell tower without straying from the meetinghouse plan. In time, however, the imitation of Anglican bell towers and spires became explicit. After completing what was to remain one of the largest meeting houses in the colony, Guilford,

Connecticut, voted in 1727 to attach a standing bell tower after the "Fashion and proportion of the Belfry and Spire at Rhode Island." The only known "Spire" in that colony was the 1726 bell tower on Trinity Church in Newport. The town later rescinded this vote and built a spire in another, unknown design, but the important breakthrough had been made.[14] Neighboring Wallingford and Milford followed with bell towers in 1728; the First Congregational in Newport and the Third Church in Boston ("Old South") in 1729; and Portsmouth, New Hampshire, in 1730. By the time Springfield, Massachusetts, built a standing bell tower in 1737 and Roxbury, Massachusetts, followed in 1741, the concept was an accepted alternative to the bell coneys that previously had been erected on the end of the straight roof.

The use of high, standing bell towers and steeples was accompanied by a new weather vane form. The gilt copper weathercock that was attached to the spire of the 1763 "Old South" in Worcester is probably typical of hundreds of such new vanes in the eighteenth century. In view of the much larger size of the weathercock compared to the earlier iron flags, it is likely that the rooster design was intended to be seen on top of a spire one hundred feet or more above the ground. Although other vane forms were to replace the weathercock, all were large. The four-foot-long gilt, copper, and iron banner vane from the fourth meeting house in Dorchester represents a late eighteenth-century weather vane form. The seven-foot shooting star vane from the 1823 Second Parish in Worcester represents a form that did not become dominant until the early nineteenth century.

Throughout the eighteenth century, urban congregations simulated other elements of the Anglican "code." When the Third Church in Boston erected the "Old South" meeting house in 1729, every window in the brick building, including the pulpit window, was designed with a rounded top in the manner of Trinity Church in Newport. As William Giles Munson's nineteenth-century townscape of New Haven reveals, the "Brick Meeting House" that replaced the second (1669) meeting house on New Haven Green in 1757 was furnished with similar windows (Figure 2).

In one or two instances, rural congregations gravitated toward religious decorative motifs that may have derived from Anglican modes. The statue of the angel Gabriel, carved from a single piece of pine, was placed in the Royalston, Massachusetts, meeting house after its completion in 1797 (Figure 125). Nineteenth-century oral tradition describes at least one Puritan pulpit (in Burrillville, Rhode Island) as having a "cherubim" painted above it.[15]

14. Kelly, 1:172.
15. Horace A. Keach, *Burrillville as It Was and as It Is* (Providence: Knowles, Anthony & Co., 1856), p. 34.

2. New Haven Green in 1800.

Concurrent with the increasing use of Anglican architectural forms was the introduction of academic or Georgian decorative motifs, such as quoins, dentil work, modillions, and pilasters; circular or half-circular windows; and broken-scroll, triangular, or flat doorway and window pediments. The dentiled cornice from a window in the second meeting house in Shrewsbury, Massachusetts, is probably representative of the kind of academic motifs commonly used in rural meeting-house architecture in the second half of the eighteenth century (Figure 60). The curved, fielded-panel casing from the pulpit window in Lempster, New Hampshire (1794), is typical of the treatment given to important interior features (Figure 61).

Contracts record the use of these motifs in a technical vocabulary. The 1788 meeting house in Warwick, Massachusetts, built by Captain Samuel Langley was to have a "roof . . . with double cornice at the gable ends, with one compass window in each gable end . . . [and]

60. *Detail of window cornice from the second meeting house in Shrewsbury, Mass., 1766.*

61. *Detail, pulpit window casing from the 1794 meeting house in Lempster, N.H.*

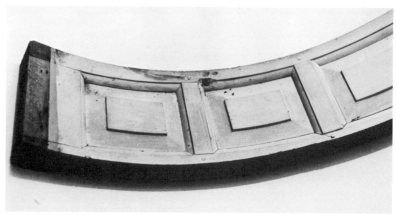

thirty-three windows." The doors were to be furnished with "architraves, cornice, and caps [pediments]"; the windows with "cornice, and solid caps." Similarly, when building its first meeting house in 1789, Dunbarton, New Hampshire, specified that its exterior was to receive a coat of "good stone color," and the structure itself was to be finished on the inside and outside in "Tuscan order." In the adoption of Georgian motifs, as elsewhere, the ever-present resistance to innovation is evident. In a 1787 vote clearly implying dissatisfaction with contemporary unrestricted use of Georgian decorative work, the South Society in Andover stipulated "nothing superfluous" for its new meeting house. Rather, it was to be "Plain and neat, not have any medallions, dentals or carved work . . ."[16]

Documentary evidence of exterior coloring or painting of meeting houses can be found as early as 1738 when Petersham, Massachusetts, paid the master builder Thomas Dick £3.10.0 for "coloring" the meeting house. "Lead color" was used on the Madison, Connecticut, meeting house in 1742; Rowley, Massachusetts, paid for "redding" its meeting house in 1744. In none of these examples is it clear whether the color was applied to the exterior clapboards or to the interior woodwork, such as the pulpit and gallery breastwork. However, on 26 April 1762, the town of Pomfret, Connecticut, voted that its large new meeting house "be colored on the outside of an orange color—the doors and bottom boards of a chocolate color—the windows, jets, cover boards and weather boards, colored white." In 1768 nearby Dudley, Massachusetts, voted to imitate Pomfret colors; in 1769 neighboring Thompson and Killingly did likewise.[17]

On the basis of similar votes, rural meeting houses after 1760 are known to have been painted yellow, orange, white, brown, blue, and green. Some were painted in combinations: yellow front with a red roof and back as in Harwich, Massachusetts (1792), or light yellow clapboards with green doors in Keene, New Hampshire (1790). Until the nineteenth century, the most common clapboard colors were "spruce yellow," "light yellow," or "yellow"; the most common roof color was "Spanish brown" (dull red). Virtually all of these colors are found in contemporary representations. The watercolor map of Rindge, New Hampshire, by Mary Kimball illustrates the red roof and yellow clapboards of the town's second meeting house, erected by the master builders John and David Barker in 1796 (Figure 38). The 1806 Wadsworth map of New Haven, which has a color code "r" (red) or "b" (blue) beside each principal building, identifies with "b" the "Blue Meeting House" of the New Light separatist group that broke with the Reverend Noyes's church during the Great Awakening reli-

16. Jonathan Blake, *History of the Town of Warwick, Massachusetts* (Boston: Noyes, 1873), p. 721; Caleb Stark, *History of the Town of Dunbarton, Merrimack County, New Hampshire* (Concord, N.H.: G. Parker Lyon), pp. 160–161; George Mooar, *Historical Manual of the South Church in Andover, Massachusetts* (Andover, Mass.: Draper, 1859), p. 32.

17. Peter Benes, "The Templeton 'Run' and the Pomfret 'Cluster': Patterns of Diffusion in Rural New England Meetinghouse Architecture, 1647–1822," *Old-Time New England* 68 (Winter–Spring 1978): 20; *150th Anniversary of the First Church in Pomfret, Connecticut* (Danielson, Conn.: Transcript Press, 1866), pp. 43–44.

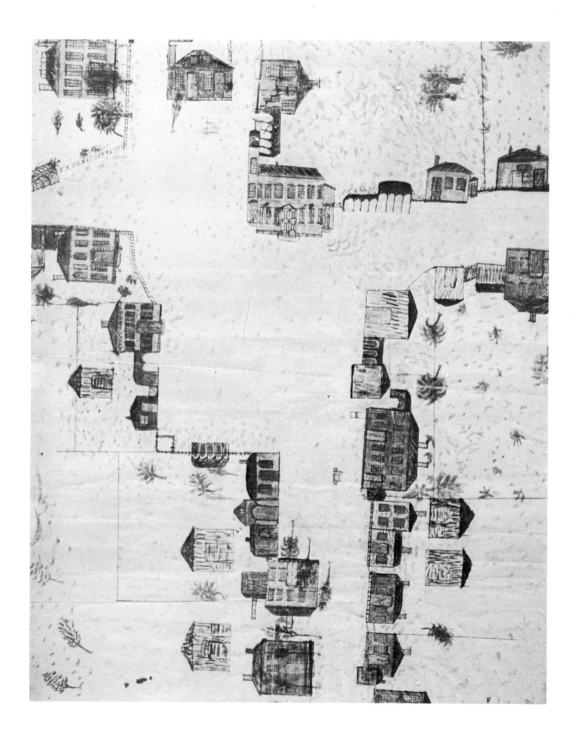

22

gious revival. In 1805 Lucy Griswold of Springfield, Massachusetts, embroidered a light brown meeting house with a reddish roof on a mourning picture (Figure 45). The ink and watercolor Joseph Joy mourning picture, made about 1812, depicts a meeting house complete with bell tower and front stairwell porch almost identical to the 1747 meetinghouse survival in Cohasset, Massachusetts (Figure 46). Its "weather boards," baseboards, and cornerboards picked out in white against green clapboards follow the pattern, though not the colors, of the 1762 Pomfret vote; the green matches a vote taken in Ashburnham, Massachusetts, in 1791 to color its meeting house a "pea green." (The town changed its mind later and painted the meeting house white.) It matches, too, a 1789 vote in Woodbury, Connecticut, that specified

38. Town of Rindge, N.H., ca. 1839.

45. Mourning picture by Lucy Griswold, Springfield, Mass., 1805.

46. Joseph Joy mourning picture, ca. 1812.

18. Josiah Paine, *History of Harwich* (Rutland, Vt.: Tuttle, 1937), p. 251; David R. Proper, *History of the First Congregational Church, Keene, N.H.* (Keene, N.H.: Sentinel, 1973), p. 40; *History of Ashburnham, Massachusetts* (Ashburnham, Mass.: privately printed, 1887), p. 285; Kelly, 2:320.
19. Norman Morrison Isham, *The Meetinghouse of the First Baptist Church in Providence: A History of the Fabric* (Providence: Charitable Baptist Society, 1925), p. 26.

"the color of the meeting-house be near the color of Mr. Tim^y Tomlinsons except it be a little more of a greenish as it."[18]

An unexpected source of color data is needlework samplers in which meeting houses and churches serve as subjects. On the basis of an itemized contract, it is known that the roof of the Baptist meeting house built in Providence in 1775 was painted "with Tar & Spannish Brown."[19] What the written record does not indicate (but what the Balch school sampler by Susan Smith, 1794, suggests quite convincingly) is that this color was not only applied to the sixty thousand shingles that made up the roof but to the interiors of the triangular pediments on the porch and gable ends (Figure 41). Although the needlework picture made by Bia Hale of the 1802 Baptist meeting house in Alstead, New Hampshire, has faded considerably, an examination of the reverse side discloses that the clapboards were sewn in beige silk, the doors and windows in blue silk, and the cornice and spire in a bright yellow silk (Figure 42). The eighteenth-century sampler by Mary Whitehead, who is thought to have lived in Middletown,

41. Sampler by Susan Smith, Rhode Island, 1793–1794.

25

20. Peter Benes, "Sky Colors and Scattered Clouds: The Decorative and Architectural Painting of New England Meeting Houses, 1738–1834," manuscript to be read at the fourth annual Dublin Seminar for New England Folklife, Dublin, New Hampshire (1979) and to appear in *Annual Proceedings of the Dublin Seminar for New England Folklife* (1979).

Connecticut, shows a blue structure that may have been a meeting house or court house (Figure 39). (The centrally mounted belfry or cupola is consistent with either interpretation.) Despite its uncertain provenance, the sampler offers critically important data because blue colors have been located on at least four meeting houses in Connecticut—in turn suggesting the possibility that meetinghouse colors (or colors of municipal buildings) followed regional groupings and that towns in central and southern Connecticut selected blue.[20]

On the basis of available evidence, the directions for the exterior painting of meeting houses after 1788 increasingly specify "stone color." The choice was no doubt deliberate and represents an attempt to simulate the building materials of classical architecture. Just as

quoins and rustication of eighteenth-century Georgian structures helped simulate dressed stone, pigments such as "light stone color," "dark stone color," or "yellow stone color"—whatever their actual appearance—contributed to the architectural deception implicit in provincial Georgian decorative motifs.

39. Sampler by Mary Whitehead, ca. 1750.

21. William G. McLouglin, *New England Dissent, 1630–1833: Baptists and the Separation of Church and State*, 2 vols. (Cambridge: Harvard University Press, 1971), pp. 894–911, 1043–1062, 1245–1262. Rhode Island, where religious toleration had been practiced since the founding of the colony in the seventeenth century, did not allow compulsory religious taxation.

22. Frederic C. Detwiller, "Thomas Dawes' Brattle Square Church," manuscript in possession of the author; *First Centenary, North Church and Society, Salem, Massachusetts* (Salem, Mass.: privately printed, 1873), pp. 22–23; Isham, pp. 24–25.

Nineteenth-Century Meeting Houses and Churches

The late eighteenth and early nineteenth centuries saw the final architectural conversion of the Puritan meeting house into a church. This conversion took place without the abandonment of the dual civic and ecclesiastical role of the structures. The legal separation of church and state and the consequent disestablishment of Congregational and Presbyterian denominations was not to take place until 1807 in Vermont, 1817 in Connecticut, 1819 in New Hampshire, and 1832 in Massachusetts.[21] The result was that for several decades and more, religious architectural forms continued to serve joint ecclesiastical and civic functions. These structures had every appearance of "churches" but were legally, and in fact, municipal meeting houses.

The shift began with the second Brattle Square Church, built of brick with brownstone quoins in 1772 after a plan designed by the architect Thomas Dawes, a member of that church. Although its spire was never completed, the building reproduced three Anglican "codes": the church plan, compass windows, and the use of the bell-tower door as the principal entry. A comparable design was used in the same year for the first meeting house of the newly formed North Church and Society in Salem, Massachusetts. Three years later in 1775, following a visit to Boston "in order to view the different churches," Joseph Brown, Comfort Wheaton, and Jonathan Hammond (respectively, architect, housewright, and joiner) built a large 80- by 80-foot meeting house for the First Baptist Society of Providence. Although the new Baptist meeting house was square in plan, the builders used the base of the bell tower as one of three principal entries and located the pulpit across the main aisle opposite the tower. As announced in the *Providence Gazette* 10 June 1775, the tower and spire were taken from "the middle Figure in the 30th Plate of Gibbs designs" (Figure 21). According to tradition, the copy of James Gibbs's *Book of Architecture* (published in London, 1728) now in the Providence Athenaeum is the one used by Joseph Brown in designing the spire. The compass windows, quoins, dentiled cornice, "ox-eye" (oculus) pediment window and "Dorrick Vernition" (Doric Venetian) pulpit window of the new meeting house were as ambitious as those found on the Brattle Square Church.[22]

Rural societies continued to build houses of worship on a meeting-house plan, either unaware of the Brattle Square, North Church, or First Baptist innovations or unwilling to adopt them. It was not until fourteen years later, in 1789, that Taunton and Pittsfield, Massachusetts—two communities removed from direct urban influence—hired

21. *Plate 30, James Gibbs's* Book of Architecture, *1728.*

14. Dublin Hill, ca. 1846.

the Boston architect Charles Bulfinch to design large, porticoed meeting houses built on a church plan. Working in a much stricter academic vocabulary derived from English architectural design books or their own American versions, Bulfinch and other architects and architect-builders rapidly developed what soon became a new dominant form. It was marked by shallow, projecting porches or porticoes, roof-supported storied steeples, Palladian windows, low-pitched roofs, and the increased use of classical orders. A prominent rural example was the Jonathan Cutting and Elias Carter meeting house in Templeton, Massachusetts (1809), which was imitated subsequently by a number of communities in southern New Hampshire. The pencil drawing of Dublin Hill made by Maria E. Perry (Figure 14) about 1846 illustrates the Templeton-type tower that was part of the second meeting house in Dublin, New Hampshire, built in 1818.[23]

23. Benes, "The Templeton 'Run' and the Pomfret 'Cluster,'" pp. 6–9.

A widely imitated urban design was prepared by the architect Asher Benjamin for the West Church in Boston, built in 1806. Appearing as Plate 39 in Benjamin's and Daniel Raynerd's *The American Builder's Companion*, published that same year, the design is notable for the pronounced projection of the central pavillion. Numerous adaptations of this design in both urban and rural buildings attest to its widespread popularity. The desire to update meetinghouse exteriors was sometimes accomplished by simply adding a new facade over the existing exterior, as in Hopkinton, New Hampshire, where the meeting house, originally a common twin-porch structure, was enlarged by means of a massive portico and steeple (Figure 11).[24]

The appearance in New England of Greek revival and Gothic revival motifs reflected a continued use of academic designs in architecture. Beginning in 1820 with the granite St. Paul's in Boston (designed by Alexander Parris and Solomon Willard) and the First Church of Quincy, 1828 (also designed by Parris), Greek revival styles steadily increased in popularity. By the 1830s most meeting houses were built after this fashion. And as with previous style innovations, many towns updated their meeting houses by applying the new motifs over the existing framework. For example, the present First Parish Church in Windsor, Connecticut (1794), which is characteristic of the Greek revival style found in a rural context, represents an 1844 adaptation in which four Doric columns were added to support a frieze, cornice, pediment, and bell tower. These features in effect serve as a Greek revival "face" for what is otherwise an eighteenth-century meeting house. With the dominance of the Greek revival style came the final phase of exterior coloring: Meeting houses that had previously been "orange color" and "chocolate color" and that more recently had been dark, light, or yellow stone color, now became universally white.

The Federal Street Church in Boston, designed by Charles Bulfinch in 1809, was the first in New England to introduce a Gothic treatment of windows, doorways, and steeple, as well as a similar treatment of interior furnishings such as the pulpit. However, these elements were simply overlaid on a Georgian foundation and did not represent a true change in style. That was not to come until the 1830s, when a serious attempt was made to understand the principles governing medieval Gothic architecture. This new style, whose English origins focus on the written work and buildings of Augustus Welby Pugin, gradually took hold in New England in the 1840s and remained a significant force for decades thereafter.

24. Asher Benjamin and Daniel Raynerd, *The American Builder's Companion* (Boston: 1806). In the second edition of this work (issued by Benjamin in Charlestown, Mass., in 1811), the West Church design appears as Plate 57; Peter Benes, "Twin-Porch *versus* Single-Porch Stairwells: Two Examples of Cluster Dispersal in Rural Meetinghouse Architecture," *Old-Time New England* 69 (Winter–Spring 1979), in press.

Congregational Meeting-House
Hopkinton N.H.
1826

Nothing is more instructive about the architectural metamorphosis
of the meeting house than the fate of survivals owned by religious
bodies after the separation of church and state in the early nineteenth
century. The "Old South" meeting house, erected during the ministry

of Thaddeus Maccarty in 1763 at a cost of £1,542, was the second house of worship of the first church in Worcester, Massachusetts. As illustrated in a nineteenth-century pen and ink sketch, the structure was furnished with a bell tower and spire and with an entry porch over its long-side door (Figure 28). Additional pews were installed in 1783 and 1805. In 1828, when the First Parish Church incorporated itself independently from the town of Worcester and assumed ownership of the building, the structure was literally converted into a

28. *1882 drawing of the Old South Church in Worcester, Mass., as it appeared in 1817.*

29. *The Old South Church in Worcester, Mass., as it appeared in 1828.*

25. Ira M. Barton, *Historical Discourse delivered at Worcester in the Old South Meeting House, September 22, 1863* (Worcester, Mass.: Edward B. Fiske, 1863), pp. 10, 12, 86; *Illustrated Business Guide of the City of Worcester, Massachusetts* (Worcester, Mass.: Snow Woodman & Co., 1881), p. 69.

church by being "turned"—meaning that the long-side entry and porch were removed, a principal entry was made through the tower, and the pulpit was placed on the short side opposite the tower. A nineteenth-century relief print reveals that a portico was added to the tower (Figure 29). In 1835 an addition of twenty-five feet was made for a vestry; in 1846 a portion of the vestry was converted into an organ loft and committee room. A later photograph made after new alterations in 1871 shows that long, tinted windows reaching floor to ceiling replaced the old sash frames (Figure 31). Finally, in 1886 the structure was torn down and replaced with a masonry one.[25]

By way of contrast, the meeting house in Washington, New Hampshire, built in 1789 as a twin-porch structure with a bell tower added later, remained in town ownership after New Hampshire's Toleration Act was passed in 1819. The Congregational church, however, continued to use it for religious services. When the church built a Gothic revival house of worship for itself in 1840, the town removed the pulpit and pews from the old meeting house and converted the gallery level into a second floor. To this day, the ground floor is used for town offices and annual town meetings, and the gallery or second floor is used as a dance hall.

Interior Furnishings

PULPITS

At the risk of oversimplifying a highly complex evolution of forms, it can be generally stated that the interior furnishings of New England meeting houses were less subject to stylistic change than the exterior or architectural elements, and less prone to mimic Anglican forms. The most dominant interior feature of the meeting house, the pulpit (also termed a "desk") was a direct architectural expression of Puritan religious practices, reflecting the emphasis of the spoken aspect of the religious service over the sacramental. Both its central location and its decorative treatment were an embodiment of the view that the primary function of religion was the dissemination of the word of God to the congregation.

Because of an absence of survivals, knowledge about seventeenth-century pulpits is limited to what can be reconstructed from fragments and from partial descriptions in seventeenth-century meetinghouse contracts. The evidence suggests that they probably resembled some English pulpits of the same time period, that they were elevated and wainscoted, that some may have been self-standing, and that most were furnished with a canopy or cover.

The early seventeenth-century parish pulpit in England was an elevated open capsule reached by a flight of stairs. Its location was off the axis of the main aisle, thus not blocking the view of the chancel. Documentary evidence uncovered in a recent study of two surviving panels from the 1656 pulpit at Medfield, Massachusetts, suggests that the pulpit was a capsule style elevated on "pilers," or posts (Figures 72a and 72b). This interpretation is reinforced by the fact that the pulpit was built in Dedham by the carpenter John Houghton and *carted* to Medfield for installation, and by the knowledge that the town of Blythborough, England, from which Houghton emigrated, has a seventeenth-century pulpit that is compatible in all respects (except the canopy) to the Medfield contract description. The contract for the 1658 Malden, Massachusetts, meeting house provided for a "pullpitt

31. The Old South Church in Worcester, Mass., after the 1871 alterations.

35

72a. Diamond-shaped carved panel from
the 1655 pulpit at Medfield, Mass.
72b. Rectangular carved panel from the
1655 pulpit at Medfield, Mass.

and cover to be of wainscott to conteyne ffive or six persons." While this description suggests a substantial pulpit, larger perhaps than those that survive in eighteenth-century meeting houses, the use of the term "conteyne" nevertheless suggests volume, hence the capsule type.[26]

A different picture emerges from the contract description of the 1681 "wainshote pulpit" in Topsfield, Massachusetts; this contract instructed the builders to make a pulpit "ten foot Long and if ye rome will giue way is to be longer & for breth as ye rome will giue way . . ." while the 1657 contract for the second meeting house in Portsmouth, New Hampshire, specified a "complete pulpet . . . to reach ye two midle posts." Both descriptions suggest a flattened, wall-attached structure rather than a freestanding capsule.[27]

By the second decade of the eighteenth century, the congruence of Puritan and Anglican pulpit design—if, indeed, it had existed during the seventeenth century—had come to an end. The three-panel pulpit front installed 1719 in the East Haven, Connecticut, meeting house is clearly part of a wall-attached type in use by Puritan churches throughout the eighteenth century (Figure 73). On the basis of later survivals at the Rocky Hill meeting house in Amesbury, Massachusetts, and at Sandown and Danville, New Hampshire, these pulpits consisted of an elevated platform fixed to the wall, a projecting front and desk supported by a base, and flanking wings that angled back and met the wall. In contrast, Anglican pulpit survivals such as those at Christ Church in Boston (1723) and Trinity Church in Newport (1726) continued the capsule tradition.

A vote taken in 1719 stipulated that the pulpit and seats in the East Haven meeting house were to have the "form of the Branford meeting house." At least two adjoining meeting houses in Connecticut, therefore, probably shared a wainscot, or joined, treatment of the pulpit rather than the "battin" (vertical plank) construction that was voted by Kensington, Connecticut, five years earlier. A similar sharing is demonstrated by the shell-form pulpit base from Southington, Connecticut, installed in the town's second meeting house about 1757, which is virtually identical to a base under the front of the 1764 pulpit in Wethersfield (Figure 75). Since the towns were located about thirteen miles from each other, it is possible that both bases were the product of the same carpenter or shop.[28]

The evidence of survivals and documentary sources indicates that pulpits were extensively colored and marbleized. At least some portions of the present Sandown, New Hampshire, mahoganized pulpit are probably original, as are the marbleized pilasters that survive in the 1785 Rocky Hill meeting house. Town records offer further proof

26. Robert Blair St. George, "Style and Structure in the Joinery of Dedham and Medfield, Massachusetts, 1635–1685," in *Winterthur Portfolio 13*, ed. Ian M. G. Quimby (Chicago: Published by the University of Chicago Press for the Henry Francis du Pont Winterthur Museum, 1979), pp. 1–46; *Bicentennial Book of Malden* (Boston: Rand, 1850), pp. 123–125.

27. *Historical Manual of the Congregational Church of Topsfield, Massachusetts 1663–1907* (Topsfield, Mass., privately printed, 1907), p. 7; Adams, *Historical Discourse, Portsmouth*, p. 25.

28. Havens, *Historical Discourse, East Haven*, p. 21; *Two-Hundredth Anniversary, Kensington Congregational Church* (Kensington, Conn., 1912), p. 37.

*73. Pulpit front from the meeting house
in East Haven, Conn., 1719.*

of these treatments. The pulpit of the Gilsum, New Hampshire, meeting house, completed in 1791, was to be a "Stone Gray" and its canopy a "Prussian Blue." The Holland, Massachusetts, pulpit was to be "colloured a good hansome pee-green." According to secondhand descriptions, the color of the canopy, pillars, and pulpit at Gilead, Connecticut, was "light red, slightly striped with white." The spiral finial from the eighteenth-century sounding board in Dorchester, the flame finial from Concord, Massachusetts, and the pineapple finial from Berlin, Massachusetts, reinforce the historical records: Carpenters lavished on the pulpit the kind of decorative treatment not found elsewhere in the meeting house (Figures 80, 81, and 82).[29]

An example of ornate decorative treatment is the pine pulpit and canopy built for the 1749 meeting house of the First Church in Ipswich, Massachusetts, by the carpenter Abraham Knowlton (Figures 74a & 74b). Like other eighteenth-century examples, the Ipswich pulpit consists of an elevated platform and desk supported by a carved

75. Shell-form pulpit base from the second meeting house in Southington, Conn., 1757.

29. Silvanus Hayward, *History of Gilsum, N.H., 1752–1859* (Manchester, N.H., privately printed, 1881), p. 102; Martin Lovering, History of Holland, Massachusetts (Rutland, Vt.: Tuttle, 1915), p. 189; Josiah A. Mack, *Historical Sketch of the Congregational Church in Gilead* (Hartford: Moseley, 1878), p. 13.

80. *Spiral finial from the fourth meeting house in Dorchester, Mass., 1743.*

81. *Flame finial from the fourth meeting house in Concord, Mass., ca. 1744.*

30. William Bentley, *The Diary of William Bentley D.D., Pastor of the East Church, Salem, Massachusetts,* 4 vols. (Salem: Essex Institute, 1905), 3:526 (21 June 1810).

shell-form base; the entirety is surmounted by a canopy. In this instance, rather than the more common vertical projection in the front such as was made in East Haven, Knowlton added a double-indented, curved front whose massing resembles the *bombé* form characteristic of some fine Boston furniture of a slightly later date. The raised lectern follows the indented frontal sections, and both the canopy and pulpit were painted to imitate mahogany. (Among the costs of the pulpit were "white lead" and "amber.") In its original setting, the pulpit was flanked by "Corinthian Gilt Capital(s)." [30]

The ambitious decorative treatment of this pulpit may have been a function of a major rift in the Ipswich community in the middle of the eighteenth century. The First Parish built its 1749 meeting house in part as a reaction to the withdrawal of a dissatisfied faction of south side residents, who built their own meeting house in 1748, a Boston carpenter being hired to make the pulpit. Sensitive to the potential

82. Pineapple finial from the first meeting house in Berlin, Mass., 1787.

41

*74a. Pulpit from the fourth meeting
house in Ipswich, Mass., 1749.*

*74b. Sounding board from the fourth
meeting house in Ipswich, Mass., 1749.*

43

31. Thomas F. Waters, *Ipswich in the Massachusetts Bay Colony*, 2 vols. (Ipswich, Mass.: Ipswich Historical Society, 1917), 2:261, 440, 473–474; Bentley, *Diary*, 3:526.
32. Lothrop, p. 101. The authors wish to thank Clinton Savage for her research regarding the identification of Mr. Crafts.

competition from the new south side group, the First Parish instructed Knowlton to spare no effort in outdoing the "unpretentious" south side pulpit, which was said to have been simply "painted white." To ensure this, a group of Ipswich subscribers, who were still members of the First Parish, contributed considerable sums privately to help pay the costs. Knowledge of the Ipswich pulpit competition was still in circulation when William Bentley visited the town in 1810. He noted in his diary that "a Mr. Knowlton entered into competition & let his pride assist this execution which was unexampled at that day."[31]

An equally ambitious pulpit was built in 1772 in the second meeting house of the Brattle Square Church, probably by William Crafts or possibly by his father, Thomas Crafts, Sr., and paid for by the merchant John Hancock of Boston (Figure 76).[32] Made of mahogany with a veneer of mahogany to mask the joinery, its decorative treatment and Corinthian setting within the church represent a full flowering of urban high-style taste in the second half of the eighteenth century. Like the Ipswich example, the pulpit front has a curved profile. Its roccoco base has some of the most ornate foliage carving to be found in New England.

The mahogany pulpit installed 1809 in the Federal Street Church in Boston is evidence that the new academic motifs that were continuing to emerge in meetinghouse and church architecture were also influencing interior furniture and fixtures (Figure 77). Like the building in which it was installed, the pulpit represents a neo-Gothic decorative application on what was still an eighteenth-century Georgian form. It points to an increasing reliance on rich mahogany veneers for surface decoration.

PULPIT CUSHIONS

An important pulpit accessory was the cushion that rested on the desk and that held the pulpit Bible or the text of the minister's sermon. Hartford, Connecticut, in 1699 ordered a "Plush Cushion, a green Cloth, and Silke for the fringes and Tasseles of sd Cushion," paying £10.14.6, a substantial sum at that time. Litchfield, Connecticut, voted in 1731 "to get a cushen or pillor for the pulpit & to be made of plush & stuft with fethers." The value of the cushion is reflected in the fact that it was one of two things saved from the "unsparing conflagration" that destroyed the 1774 meeting house of the Tabernacle Church in Salem, Massachusetts. However, the cushion may not have been there initially for the express purpose of holding the Bible. For example, the church records of Sandwich, Massachusetts, reveal that

*76. Pulpit front from the Brattle Square
Church, Boston, Mass., 1772.*

45

*77. Pulpit from the Federal Street
Church, Boston, Mass., 1809.*
46

the church voted to "read Scriptures on Lord's Days" in 1754—strong evidence that they had *not* been read prior to this. Comparable votes are found in the years from 1736 to 1775, many of them precipitated by the gift of a Bible contingent on its being read from the pulpit. The "pulpit Bible," therefore, may have been a later tradition in New England's religious history than the cushion that presumably held it.[33]

PULPIT HOURGLASSES

An hourglass was often placed on a stand or on the pulpit within view of both the minister and the congregation. Published sermons suggest a delivery time consistent with one or two turns of the glass. Samuel Sewall's *Diary* gives further insight. At age twenty-three, Sewall preached in place of Thomas Parker and in his anxiety neglected to time himself: "Being afraid to look on the glass, ignorantly and unwittingly I stood two hours and a half."

Most likely, a sexton or deacon turned the glass as the minister read. In the Woodstock, Connecticut, Congregational Church the hourglass was set into an iron stand, now known only by a glass-plate negative, which was probably made in the early eighteenth century (Figure 111). (The hourglass that still survives as part of the church's property probably replaced an earlier hourglass, since its mahogany frame suggests a time of manufacture later in the century.) The appearance of the Woodstock stand supports a tradition circulating in Wilmington, Massachusetts, in the nineteenth century that "an iron bracket, shaped like a crane" held the hourglass at the minister's right hand. A tradition of an "iron frame" is associated with the Presbyterian meeting house in Londonderry, New Hampshire. The vote taken in Amesbury, Massachusetts, in 1762, however, which ordered Samuel Blasdell to make a "settle at the pulpit for the hourglass to stand in"—suggests a holder made out of wood that also served as a container. By the turn of the century, many parishes replaced their hourglasses with wall clocks. Typically, these clocks were mounted on the front of the gallery facing the pulpit.[34]

PEWS

Despite a greater number of survivals, the same obscurity that surrounds seventeenth-century pulpits also surrounds seventeenth-century pews. The paneled oak pew door and pew section made for the first Marblehead, Massachusetts, meeting house on Burial Hill in 1659 by the joiner John Norman were later used in the town's second

33. Kelly, 1:194, 275; Samuel M. Worcester, *A Memorial of the Old and New Tabernacle, Salem, Mass.* (Boston: Crocker & Brewster, 1855), p. 18; *Sandwich Church Records*, p. 64, Library of the New England Historic Genealogical Society, Boston, Mass.

34. Samuel Sewall, *Diary, 1674–1729*, ed. M. Halsey Thomas, 2 vols. (New York: Farrar, Straus & Giroux, 1973), 1:11; *History, Yearbook and Church Directory. Arthur A. Simmons, Minister* (Wilmington, Mass.: First Congregational Church, [1933]), unpaged; Edward L. Parker, *History of Londonderry, N.H.* (Boston: Perkins & Whipple, 1851), p. 153; Joseph Merrill, *History of Amesbury* (Haverhill, Mass.: Stiles, 1880), p. 236.

111. Photograph of the hourglass frame from the meeting house in Woodstock, Conn. Early eighteenth century.

35. "Marblehead Town Records," annotated by William H. Bowden, *Essex Institute Historical Collections* 69 (July–October 1933):226. Two additional pew sections made by John Norman were recently discovered by Robert F. Trent in a three-story Federal house in Marblehead, Massachusetts, where they had been reused as paneling.

meeting house, built in 1695 (Figures 85a and 85b). The height of these sections (38½ inches) indicates a shift away from the "high" pews of sixteenth-century English experience; and indeed a reconstruction of the appearance of the complete (approximately 5-foot square) pew from two additional surviving sections made by the same joiner is consistent with a size that was to remain constant until the nineteenth century.[35]

Documentary references to pews, however, are much more ambiguous. According to the 1661 town records of Windsor, Connecticut, William Buel of that town was ordered "to alter the great pew into two, one part for the magistrates, and one for other, and that it be raised equal with short seats." A "great pew" was probably two or three times normal size and its elevation and division may have been a way of conferring dignity on the magistrates. In a 1672 vote taken

85b. Pew end from the first meeting house in Marblehead, Mass., 1659.

85a. Pew door from the first meeting house in Marblehead, Mass., 1659.

49

36. Kelly, 2:304; Adams, *Historical Discourse, Portsmouth* pp. 25, 35; Samuel A. Bates, ed., *Records of the Town of Braintree, 1640 to 1793* (Randolph, Mass.: D. H. Huxford, 1886), p. 36.

in Portsmouth, New Hampshire, "Nehemiah Partridge and five or six more people have free liberty to build a payre of stayres up to the westward beame within the meetinghouse and a pew upon the beame." While this information helps confirm the usual size of seventeenth-century pews (pew rights in the eighteenth century were typically granted to groups of six individuals), the location of a pew "upon the beame" of a meeting house with a sixteen-foot plate height and a "flat Ruff" lends weight to the belief that as much variety may have existed in seventeenth-century pew locations as in seventeenth-century meetinghouse architecture. A similar "beame" pew was permitted in Braintree, Massachusetts, in 1697.[36]

Allowing for differences in material, in the attenuation of the turned spindles, and in the design of the panels, the open-top form represented by the 1659 Marblehead example was probably the principal pew type in New England during the period from 1670 to 1800. Pew door number 23 from the 1793 meeting house at Bolton, Massachusetts, like the box pew from the 1784 meeting house at Ludlow, Massachusetts (installed about 1799), is a late representation of the type (Figures 87 and 84). They are similar to extant pew doors and pew sides from late eighteenth-century meetinghouse survivals at Jaffrey, Lempster, Fremont, Sandown, and Danville, New Hampshire; and Alna, Maine.

The pew door number XIII from the 1828 alteration of the 1771 meeting house in Farmington, Connecticut, represents what, after a certain point, may have been a concurrent pew and slip or bench design (Figure 88). The unopened or solid form was noticeably shorter than the open-top kind and apparently lasted well into the nineteenth century. The slip end from the First Parish Church in Plymouth probably derived from the solid form (Figure 89). Stylistic updating is visible in the curvature of the top rail, which matches the shape of arms on many rocking chairs, benches, and armchairs of the Windsor type made at this time.

Common pew accessories included armrests, writing arms, footstools, and foot warmers. The wooden elbow rest from the York area of Maine represents a pedestal form of this accessory (Figure 95). The branded nineteenth-century armrest from the Wethersfield area of Connecticut suggests the form of a footstool which was adapted for this specific use (Figure 96). The hinged writing arm from the third meeting house of the First Parish in Ipswich (1749) is designed to be attached to a pew side; similar arms still exist in place in the pews of the Rocky Hill meeting house in Amesbury and in many others.

87. *Pew door from the 1793 meeting house in Bolton, Mass.*

84. Box pew from the meeting house in Ludlow, Mass., ca. 1795.

88. 1828 pew door from the 1771 meeting house in Farmington, Conn.

52

89. *Pew door from the fourth meeting house in Plymouth, Mass., 1831.*

95. Arm rest used in the First Parish meeting house, York, Maine. Eighteenth century.

96. Arm rest used in the Wethersfield, Conn., meeting house. Nineteenth century.

"Seating" the Meeting House

37. *History of the Connecticut Valley in Massachusetts*, 2:966.
38. Edwin Martin Stone, *History of Beverly* (Boston: J. Munroe & Co., 1843), pp. 251–252.

Installing seats and pews in the meeting house was much simpler than determining who was going to sit in them. In keeping with the Reformed practice of segregating men and women in the congregation, the New England meeting house had a "men's side" and "men's stairs" on the one hand, and a "women's side" and "women's stairs" on the other. Boys between ten and twenty-one, indentured servants, black slaves, and the town poor were relegated upstairs. As pews increasingly supplanted early seats and benches as the dominant seating mode in the meeting house, a concomitant pressure was exerted on the town to "seat men and women together in the pews"—meaning to allow those families wealthy enough to afford pews to have the added privilege of sitting together. This change did not take place automatically, and the decision to seat men and women together (for example, made in the Fifth Parish of Springfield, Massachusetts, in 1753) was an important break with tradition.[37]

The assignment of specific seating positions was a complex social and political task that involved the naming of a seating committee, the designation of the relative dignity of each seat in the meeting house, and the determination of the rules by which the dignity of every parishioner and his family was to be measured. Any of these decisions could be—and often was—challenged by townspeople in the town meetings. The most favored pews were those on the wall in line with the pulpit; and in some instances (particularly later on in the eighteenth century), those near the doorways. The 1682 rules for seating the second meeting house in Beverly, Massachusetts, are among the most detailed of the extant descriptions of the process of determining who was to have these pews. According to a system of ranking devised by Colonel Hale of Beverly, this system provided

> That every male be allowed one degree for every complete year of his age he exceeds twenty-one.
>
> That he be allowed for a captain's commission twelve degrees; for lieutenant's, eight degrees, and for an ensign's four degrees.
>
> That he be allowed three degrees for every shilling for real estate in the last parish tax. . . .
>
> Every generation of predecessors heretofore living in this town, to make one degree for every male descendant that is seated. That parentage be regarded no farther otherwise than to turn the scale between competition for the same seat.[38]

39. Edward E. Atwater, *History of New Haven Colony* (New York: W. W. Munsell & Co., 1887), p. 542; Kelly, 1:306.
40. Henry Allen Hazen, *History of Billerica, Massachusetts* (Boston: A. Williams & Co., 1883), p. 169.

The social implications of this and similar documents are profound and provide insight into the values that society placed not only on age and property but on extended residence in the town: The scale is clearly weighted against newcomers. Notably missing in the Beverly rules is any mention of ecclesiastical status, for example, church membership. This is a significant omission, and the Beverly example might well shed light on the presumed theocratic structure of seventeenth-century Puritan society. Much the same omission can be inferred from the 1647 seating chart of the New Haven congregation, in which church members are identified by the prefix "Bro." or "Sister." Both the men's and the women's side were seated heterogeneously—church members mixed with nonmembers: In fact, no male church members were assigned to the first three seats. An equally revealing rule is the one adopted in 1705 by Milford, Connecticut, that "no person be seated lower than his place now," suggesting the same bias against newcomers found earlier in Beverly.[39]

Raising

One of the most important civic occasions associated with the New England meeting house was the act of raising its frame—a chronological milestone in the life of the town that set apart those "present at the raising" from those who came after. The 1694 raising of the first meeting house in Billerica, Massachusetts, was recorded by the town clerk in terms suggesting that these events may not have been too different from those a hundred years later. On the appointed day (July 16) "all persons capable of labor" were summoned at seven in the morning by the "second beat of the drum."

> The service was atended upon the day apointed by about forty and five hands of our towne the first day, and the towne generally came together the second day, and many other out of other Towns, sum that came to inspect us and several that were helpful to us . . . no considerable harm done, not a bone broken; we had the helpe of our Reverend pastour to desire god's blessing and protection, and when we had finished our work we concluded with a psalm of praise and returning thanks unto god by our Reverend pastour.[40]

In the eighteenth century, a barrel of rum, hard cider, or gin was commonly provided at these occasions, and was in part a calculated means of attracting and reimbursing workers and in part a means of generating festival atmosphere. To cite only a few of many hundreds of known examples: Two barrels of "W.I. [West Indian] Rum" were used at Temple, New Hampshire; one barrel of rum at Wilton, New Hampshire; three barrels "of good Beare" at Sheffield, Massachusetts. And, in time, rum was supplemented by a communal meal or supper. The raising of the second meeting house in Newfields, New Hampshire, in 1792, occasioned the purchase of

60 gallons good West India Rum
3 Quintals of fish
3 Bbls Cyder
1 Bbl cyder "provided by Mrs. Drown"
7 Bushels Potatoes
75 lbs Butter
12 lbs Coffee
¼ C (hundredweight) Sugar[41]

41. James H. Fitts, *History of New-fields, N.H.* (Concord, N.H.: Rumford, 1912), p. 315.

Warning

Since the primary purpose of a meeting house was to provide a suitable place for the inhabitants of the parish to meet, an important responsibility of the precinct authorities of the parish was to warn the people when to assemble on lecture and sabbath days and for town or parish meetings. The term *warning* is itself suggestive; on the one hand, townspeople were warned, in the sense of being informed, that a meeting was at hand. On the other, they were advised to protect their rights as freemen and town residents or to exercise their responsibilities, which could be done only through personal participation in the town meeting.

In the period from 1630 to 1850, New England meetings were warned by a variety of means, which included drums, trumpets, flags, bells, and West Indian conches. The choice was a parish decision, and in some instances it was reviewed every year. In the seventeenth and early eighteenth centuries, drums were common in the Connecticut River Valley and probably in other regions, too. Like its counterparts in Windsor, Hartford, and New Haven, the warning drum used in Farmington, Connecticut, in the seventeenth century was beaten by the same individual who swept the meetinghouse floor, locked its doors, and rang the bell (Figure 116). In 1660 "goodman Edwards" of Wethersfield, Connecticut, received £2.5 for performing all these services. He apparently performed his job with the drum so well that the town voted the following year "that the Bell should be rung noe more

*116. Drum used in Farmington, Conn.
Seventeenth century.*

58

to call the Assembly together, on the Sabbath and Lecture days, but that the Drum should be beaten at such times."[42]

Sometimes the drum was used alternately with a trumpet, as in Windsor, Connecticut. In 1658 the town voted to make "provision upon the top of the meeting-house, from the Lanthorn [cupola] to the ridge of the house, to walk conveniently, to sound a trumpet or drum to give warning to meetings." This vote gives credence to the traditional story that drums were beaten from the vantage point of a turret or platform built at the peak of the roof. However, society meetings were also "warned by beating the Drum round the Town."[43]

According to several nineteenth-century historians, whose statements can be verified by town records, another common means of warning the meeting was to raise a red flag on a staff fixed to the meeting house. A more unusual device, apparently favored in the Connecticut River Valley north of Springfield, Massachusetts, was the conch or "cunk," which when blown correctly sounds like a horn. Stockbridge, Sunderland, and Whately, Massachusetts, records indicate that conches were used to warn meetings in these towns until the mid or late eighteenth century. Whately voted *not* to "improve" anyone to blow its conch shell in 1795. Presumably this shell had been in use since the erection of the town's first meeting house in 1773 (Figure 117). However, if Whately was satisfied with this manner of signaling the meeting, neighboring Sunderland clearly was not. Having tried a flag, the town voted to beat a drum from 1737 to 1740, reverted to a flag from 1740 to 1742, went back to a drum from 1742 to 1745, tried a "cunk shell" in 1745, returned to a drum from 1745 to 1754, and finally purchased a bell in 1754.[44]

Bells

A common means of summoning the inhabitants was by the tolling of a bell. Bells can be dated from the earliest period of English settlements in New England.[45] Suspended on coneys or cupolas located on the roof of the meeting house, these bells were typically imported from England. Often the necessary funds, or the bells themselves, were donated by individuals. Such beneficence enabled Sandwich, Massachusetts, to acquire its first bell, which was installed about 1708 (Figure 56). Cast in 1675 by a Dutch maker, this bell was the gift of the widow of a shipwrecked sea captain who lost his life together with

42. Sherman W. Adams and Henry R. Stiles, *The History of Ancient Wethersfield*, facsimile of 1904 ed. (Wethersfield, Conn.: Wethersfield Historical Society, 1974), p. 223.

43. *Quarter Millennial Anniversary of yᵉ Ancient Church in Windsor, Conn.* (Hartford: Case, Lockwood & Brainard, 1880), p. 56; Kelly, 1:308.

44. James M. Crafts, *History of Whately, Mass.* (Orange, Mass.: Crandall, 1899), p. 161; John Montague Smith, *History of Sunderland, Massachusetts* (Greenfield, Mass.: E. A. Hall, 1899), p. 161.

45. Hartford, Connecticut, installed a bell in 1639; Cambridge, Massachusetts, by 1643; Springfield, Massachusetts, in 1644; Dedham, Massachusetts, in 1651; and Wethersfield, Connecticut, by 1657. Kelly, 1:193; Lucius R. Paige, *History of Cambridge, Massachusetts, 1630–1877* (Boston, 1877), p. 258; Donnelly, pp. 122–124, 45; *The Early Records of the Town*, ed. D. G. Hill (Dedham, Mass.: Dedham Transcript, 1886–1936), 1:186–187; Adams and Stiles, *History of Ancient Wethersfield*, p. 223.

117. Conch shell used in Whately, Mass., 1773–1795.

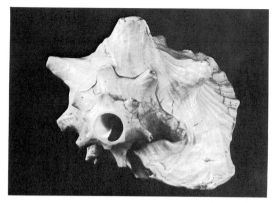

56. Bell from the second meeting house in Sandwich, Mass., 1703.

60

his crew off Sandwich in 1703. Its date makes it the earliest bell known to survive with a New England history.[46]

Bells were expensive—the first bell used in Beverly, Massachusetts, was booty seized by a Massachusetts raiding expedition against the Catholic friary at Port Royal in 1656 and donated by the commander. Like the meeting house, bells were a source of pride in the community. It is not surprising, then, to find towns imitating each other's bells, just as they imitated each other's architectural details. In 1724 Guilford, Connecticut, which two years later was to imitate "the Fashion and proportion of the Belfry & Spire at Rhode Island," voted to apply £35 toward the purchase of a bell "like that in Mr. Coleman's meeting house in Boston." The choice was not necessarily a sound one: This was the same bell that tolled of its own accord during the earthquake of 1727.[47]

Because of their weight, bells had to be secured firmly and aligned so that when they were tolled their shifting weight could be absorbed by the belfry and tower. Guilford's bell problems continued: After mounting its bell on a new 120-foot bell tower and spire, the town was obliged in 1732 to direct that "the Bell frame shall be Turned so as to have the Bell Swing east and West; the better to prevent the rocking of the Meeting House." Occasionally, other towns had to "do Something to Secure the Meeting House from Racking."[48] For this reason, some eighteenth-century parishes continued the seventeenth-century practice of hanging bells in low, covered frames or belfrys standing on the ground at a short distance from the meeting house proper. The Doolittle engraving reveals a small windowless bell coney to the right of the 1713 meeting house (Figure 20).

Like all practices associated with early New England meeting houses, the times at which the bell was rung were subject to the decision of the parish. The evidence of several votes taken in the eighteenth century indicates that bells were rung between two and four times per day to mark the hour. These times varied from town to town, and sometimes from year to year within a town. As the years progressed, the bellman's duties were increasingly replaced by the movement and striking works that were installed in New England meeting houses in the eighteenth and nineteenth centuries. The mechanism made by Daniel Burnap for the tower clock of the Suffield, Connecticut, meeting house (1786–1836) has wood and metal components, though others are known to have been made entirely out of wood (Figure 66). The sandstone clock weight—the broken-off top section of a flood height marker erected in 1801—used during the nineteenth century in the meeting house in Windsor, Connecticut,

46. This bell is known in Sandwich, Massachusetts, as the "Adolphe" bell, so-called after Captain Peter Adolphe de Groot, a Dutch immigrant, whose widow, Janeke, donated the bell to the town. See papers on file at the Sandwich Historical Society, Sandwich, Massachusetts.

47. Stone, p. 250; Kelly, 1:172.

48. Kelly, 1:173, 327.

66. *Clock mechanism from the 1786 belfry of the Suffield, Conn., meeting house.*

49. Sidney Perley, *Historic Storms of New England* (Salem: Salem Press, 1891), pp. 159–160.

shows that considerable power was required to drive these mechanisms as well as the striking works (Figure 67). The marker itself tells a story: The "Freshet of 1801" consisted of four days of rain and storm from March 18 through March 21 and caused the greatest flood ever known in some sections of New England.[49]

This
Monument
is erected in
Memory of the
Great Flood
on March 21st
A.D. 1801.

This head

50. Stiles, *History of Ancient Windsor*, p. 151; Charles A. Hazlett, *History of Rockingham County, New Hampshire, and Representative Citizens* (Chicago: Richmond-Arnold, 1915), p. 161; William Goold, *Portland in the Past* (Portland, Me.: B. Thurston & Co., 1886), p. 296; Waters, 2:443.

51. *Records of the Town of Braintree*, ed. Samuel A. Bates (Randolph, Mass.: D. H. Huxford, 1886), p. 36; Daniel B. Cutter, *History of the Town of Jaffrey, N.H. 1749–1880* (Concord, N.H.: Republican, 1881), p. 64; Frederick H. Dole, *Windham in the Past* (Auburn, Me.: Merrill, 1916), p. 116.

Discipline

As soon as it had been raised and covered, the meeting house became the site for erecting public cages, the pillory, the stocks, and the whipping post. Like the display of wolves' heads (which were nailed to the meeting house by seventeenth-century bounty hunters), these customs were a direct transplant of established English practices. William Buell, who had altered the "Great Pew" in the Windsor meeting house in 1661, the previous year had been paid "for a pair of stocks." Portsmouth, New Hampshire, ordered in 1662 that "a kage be made for the unruly and those who sleep in meeting or take tobacco on the Lord's Day out of the meeting in time of public exercise."

Court trials were usually held in the meeting house of the parish where the crime was committed, as the diaries of Samuel Sewall, Joshua Hempstead, and Matthew Patten attest. Two murder trials—the Goodwin trial in 1772 and the Thomas Bird trial in 1790—were undertaken at the Falmouth First Parish meeting house (now Portland, Maine). Both resulted in executions. So popular were these trials that special provisions had to be made to accommodate the crowds. Before Pomp, a condemned black murderer, was brought to the Ipswich meeting house in chains to hear the minister, Levi Frisbie, preach his funeral sermon, the town hired Joseph Lord to shore up the galleries.[50]

Public Notices

The meeting house also served as an exchange and dissemination point for news and vital communications. Braintree, Massachusetts, voted in 1715 "that the Publishments of Marriages for the future [are] to be set up upon the foreside of the most Publick Doors of the meeting house in said Town." In time, the "Publick Doors" were replaced by a specialized accessory that was attached near the door. The Beverly notice box probably differs only in detail from the "box . . . with a glass door" that Jaffrey, New Hampshire, ordered attached to the outside of its meeting house in 1792 "for the purpose of putting the town Notifications into" (Figure 114). These boxes continued to serve their public use even after the separation of church and state. The town clerk of Windham, Maine, posted banns in a box attached to the town's 1790 meeting house well into the nineteenth century, though it was a "source of unfeigned curiosity to all comers young and old."[51]

Public signposts served a similar purpose. When its second meeting house was erected at a new location in 1786, Plainfield, Connecticut,

114. Meetinghouse notice box.
Massachusetts, late eighteenth century.

ordered "that the Sign Post in this Town be removed from the place where it now stands, to the most convenient place on the Lot of Land lately purchased . . . for a Meeting House Lot in this Town . . ."[52]

52. Kelly, 2:133.

Tithing

Sabbath Breakers, a broadside printed by James Franklin of Boston, is an eighteenth-century copy of an earlier English broadside warning of the consequences of violating or disrupting the Puritan sabbath (Figure

Divine EXAMPLES of GOD's Severe JUDGMENTS
UPON
SABBATH BREAKERS.
In their unlawful Sports, Collected out of several Divine Subjects,
VIZ.
Mr. H. B. Mr. Beard, and the Practice of Piety: A fit Monument for our present Times, &c.

The Prophane Israelite that gathered Sticks upon the Sabbath Day, is Ston'd to Death.

Several Young Men playing at Foot-ball on the Ice on the Lords Day, are all Drown'd.

A Woman and her two Daughters spill and dry Flax on the Lords Day, are all Burnt.

A Millers House and Mill Burnt, &c.

J.F. Sculp.

FINIS.

Boston in New-England: Re-Printed and Sold in Newbury-Street.

127. *"Sabbath Breakers" broadside printed in Boston, Mass., 1718.*

127). As the survival of tithing sticks and a litany of votes directing tithingmen and other adults to curb what the 1760 town records call the "wretched boys" amply indicate, these warnings were not always heeded. A complaint made in 1673 against Thomas Mentor of Ipswich, Massachusetts, alleged that "he carried himself very irreverently and most unchristianly upon the Sabbath days in the time of worship." In particular, he annoyed the congregation "by taking of maids by the aprons as they came in to the meeting house in the time of worship, by putting his hand in their bosoms, and then taking or snatching away their posies or flowers, by laughing and allmost all the time of worship whispering with those that are like himself . . ." The following year, a man who noisily complained during prayer of the constantly shuffling feet of a neighbor was made to wear a sign "FOR DISTURBING YE MEETING" and to stand on exhibit during the next public lecture.[53]

The use of rods, sticks, and wands to handle such disorders is clearly established by votes like the one taken in 1672 in Hatfield, Massachusetts, which stipulated that "there shall be some sticks set up in the meeting house in several places, with some fit persons placed by them, to use them as occasion shall require to keep the youth from disorder." More than a hundred years later in 1796, Plainfield, Massachusetts, set aside money for "wands for the tythingmen." The funnel-ended tithing stick from the Rocky Hill parish in Wethersfield, Connecticut, confirms the traditional description of such sticks as being long and having a "ball" at one end and a "feather" at the other (Figure 119).[54] The numerous holes drilled into the cone of the funnel may well have held individual feather quills. The four-foot wooden tithing stick from Walpole, New Hampshire, also shares some of the long-stick characteristics, and in this case has a ball end (Figure 120).

A reading of Massachusetts laws gives a different picture. According to the General Provincial Laws of Massachusetts of 1698, tithing rods used in Massachusetts meeting houses were to consist of a "staffe of two foot long tip't . . . with brass."[55] The maple tithing stick from Bolton, Massachusetts, which has no known meetinghouse association, matches this description in both its length and its brass-tipped end. Not widely known or recognized today, the rod type of tithing stick may in fact have been more common than the knob- or feather-ended long kind, passing into civic use by the town's constable after its meetinghouse days were over.

A less-known source of public nuisance was the use of tobacco, which was chewed, snuffed, and smoked in significant quantity. Wethersfield, Connecticut, passed an ordinance that required "all persons

53. Waters, 2:3.
54. Arthur H. Tucker, "Hope Atherton and His Times," *Pocumtuck Valley Memorial Association Proceedings* 7 (1926): 389–390; Charles N. Dyer, *History of the Town of Plainfield, Hampshire County, Mass.* (Northampton, Mass.: Gazette, 1891), p. 32.
55. *The Acts and Resolves of the Province of Massachusetts Bay*, Vol. 1, 1692–1714 (Boston: Wright & Potter, 1869), p. 329:

Which tythingmen shall have a black staffe of two foot long, tip't at one end with brass about three inches, as a badge of their office to be provided by the Selectmen, at the charge of the town. (1698, Chapter 10, Section 7)

119. Detail, wooden tithing stick used in the meeting house in Rocky Hill, Conn., ca. 1800.

120. Tithing stick used in Walpole, N.H. Eighteenth or early nineteenth century.

102. Spit box believed to have been made for the second meeting house in Berlin, Mass., built 1826.

56. Adams and Stiles, *History of Ancient Wethersfield*, p. 234; Properties & Sexton to 1849, Box 1, Charitable Baptist Society Records, Rhode Island Historical Society Library, Providence, R.I.; bill of sale submitted by Amory Sawyer of Berlin, 1826, Box 14, Town Archives, Berlin, Mass.

who have made use of tobacco the present season during the time they have occupied their slips, [to] be requested to cleanse the same at the time they leave them." Among the itemized duties of the sexton at the First Baptist Church in Providence was to keep spitboxes "sanded & . . . in Decent order." The town of Berlin, Massachusetts, bought two spitboxes for 17 cents each after completing its new meeting house in 1828; one of these has survived (Figure 102).[56]

The Church

The first Puritan settlers who came to New England brought with them a strong tradition of religious reform. They were active participants in the continuing efforts of English Protestants to cleanse further the Christian experience of "popery." In this they were guided by the Bible, which they considered to be the sole and sufficient word of God, and they vowed to "oppose all contrarie wayes, cannons and constitutions of men in his worship."[57] While still in England, the Puritans took issue with the Reformed Church of England (est. 1559). They declared that the Anglican church had not gone far enough in its reforms, and they refused to abide by some of its tenets. Significantly, however, they still considered themselves a part of the Anglican church and sought only to "purify" it, unlike the Plymouth, Massachusetts, Pilgrims who had separated from it.

In America, the Puritans encountered few restrictions governing the substance or practice of their ideas. They were acutely aware of their opportunity, and they set forth consciously to establish a model community. The foundation of this experiment was their covenant with God—a pledge that bound together individuals who had examined one another and found visible evidence of God's grace, which manifested itself in a conversion experience. The direct consequence of this gathering was the formation of a church: "We Covenant with the Lord and one with an other; and doe bynd our selves in the presence of God, to walke together in all his waies, according as he is pleased to reveale himself unto us in his Blessed word of truth."[58]

In this manner Salem, Massachusetts, became the site in 1629 of the first Puritan church organized in America. Embodied in this and the covenants of later churches was the understanding that the authority by which each church was established came from the covenant itself and that the faith of church members alone was a sufficient sign of a true church. Puritans rejected the notion of an episcopacy or any other kind of centralized control as practiced in the Church of England, since this authoritarian body was not specifically sanctioned by the Bible.[59] Nevertheless, they required a sense of fraternity and recognition from neighboring parishes. They often consulted their neighbors in religious matters and sent their minister or another delegate to "assist in" ordinations (or dismissals) of neighboring ministers.[60]

Once a church had been gathered, it extended a "call to office" to a suitable, educated, and orthodox candidate. If he accepted, and if

57. From the second Salem Covenant (1636) reproduced in full in Williston Walker, *The Creeds and Platforms of Congregationalism* (1893; reprint ed., Boston: Pilgrim Press, 1969), pp. 116–118.
58. Walker, p. 116.
59. The formation of the First Church in Salem is outlined in Walker, pp. 102–106; David D. Hall, *The Faithful Shepherd: A History of the New England Ministry in the Seventeenth Century* (New York: W. W. Norton & Co., 1974), pp. 28–30; Sydney E. Ahlstrom, *A Religious History of the American People* (New Haven: Yale University Press, 1972), p. 132.
60. A list of such visitations to other towns appears under the date 27 April 1745 in *Plymouth Church Records, 1620–1859*, 2 vols. (Baltimore: Genealogical Publishing Co., 1975), 1:297–298.

61. First Parish Church of Portland, Maine, *Baptism, Marriage, and Death Records, 1734–1907*, 5 vols., 1:134 (26 August 1776). Manuscript at the Maine Historial Society, Portland, Me.

the secular parish or society voted to support him, he was ordained. Considering the number of ministers who served New England congregations, dismissals were rare, though they did represent an effective control over the minister's performance. In general, however, ministers faithfully discharged their duties, and some stand out as particularly noteworthy and respected town figures. Certainly, Samuel Deane of the First Parish Church in Portland, Maine, was one. He demonstrated his sympathies when he donated his entire salary for 1775 and part of his salary for 1776 to his church when the "late destruction of the town" put a financial strain on the society's ability to pay him.[61] His generosity was later rewarded when representatives of the congregation presented him with a silver mug (Figure 153). Similar sentiments were also shown when the Reverend William Brattle gave a silver baptismal

153. Silver mug presented to the Reverend Samuel Deane, Portland, Maine, in 1775.

basin, formerly a gift to him from his Harvard College students, to his "Dearly beloved Flock," the First Parish in Cambridge, Massachusetts (Figure 142).

While the Congregational "Churches of Christ," as they were called, dominated New England in the seventeenth century, other denominations coexisted, though at the cost of political and economic persecution, except in Rhode Island. Baptists, whose New England roots go back to Roger Williams's settlement in Providence, Rhode Island, represented a further removal from Anglicanism than did Congregationalists. Although all did not ascribe to the same beliefs, Baptists in general denied the validity of infant baptism, espousing instead total immersion of adults. Quakers also prospered in Rhode Island. They too carried the Reformed tradition further than Congregationalists by embracing the power of individual revelation of Scripture. This circumvented the Puritan practice of step-by-step preparation for salvation through a "Covenant of Grace" enjoyed by "visible saints." In the eighteenth century the religious climate became still more diversified,

62. Walker, p. 473; Richard L. Bushman, *From Puritan to Yankee: Character and the Social Order in Connecticut 1670–1765* (New York: W. W. Norton & Co., 1967), p. 153.
63. David S. Lovejoy, *The Glorious Revolution in America* (New York: Harper & Row, 1972), pp. 128, 348.
64. For references to these events see *The Diary of Samuel Sewall*, 1:116 (30 May 1686), 128 (21 December 1686), 142 (12 June 1687), 162–163 (28 March 1688). In 1777 South Church used King's Chapel for services because its own building had been converted into a riding school by the British army.

with the appearance of Anabaptists ("re-baptizers"), Presbyterians, Catholics, Jews, and Shakers.

Meanwhile, Congregationalism did not stagnate but continued to evolve and diversify. In the seventeenth century it withstood the internal pressures generated by the Antinomian Crisis involving Anne Hutchinson in 1637 and the events leading up to the Half-way Covenant in 1662, which extended the privilege of baptism to the children of baptized but "unregenerate" Christians. But by the end of the century, new ideas began to challenge mainstream Puritan theology. Arminianism, which questioned the Calvinist doctrine of absolute predestination, was introduced at Harvard College and spread throughout New England as Harvard's graduates became ministers. Congregationalism was fragmented still further into New and Old Light churches in the aftermath of the Great Awakening of 1740–1741, which set an emotional religious experience against the orthodox disciplined order. Finally, throughout this period, standards for admission to church membership were gradually relaxed, and a greater portion of the congregation enjoyed a voice in church affairs.[62]

Pressures from outside weakened the dominant role of Congregationalism in the religious and social life of New England. Perhaps the most significant event was the revocation of the Massachusetts Bay Charter in 1684. The charter, with the privileges and independence it granted the colony, had always been regarded as a sure sign of God's favor toward the New England way. However, in 1686 both a royal governor and the Church of England were introduced into Boston. When the colony was given a new charter in 1691, the office of royal governor stayed, voting privileges were tied to property instead of membership in a Puritan church, and "liberty of conscience" was guaranteed to all Christians except Catholics.[63]

While the Puritans had never formally separated from the Anglican church, neither had they conformed to many of its practices. The difference between them became apparent when, for example, the newly arrived Church of England requested the use of one of the Boston meeting houses for worship. The Boston congregations responded that they "could not with a good conscience consent that our Meeting Houses should be made use of for the Common-Prayer Worship." Shortly thereafter, South Church was forced to share its meeting house with the Anglican church, and both services were held there until the first King's Chapel was completed in 1689.[64]

The tensions between Congregationalists and Anglicans eased during the eighteenth century, in part because the differences between the two sects became less pronounced. Aside from growing similarities between meeting houses and churches, Congregationalism assumed a more institutionalized structure. A clear step in this direction was taken by the Connecticut churches that adopted the Saybrook Platform in 1708. Aimed at promoting church discipline, this "ecclesiastical constitution" united neighboring churches into "consociations" and strengthened the legal authority of the ministry.[65] Moreover, occasional parish votes, like that at Plymouth, Massachusetts, in 1770, went beyond mere toleration and showed a willingness to share communion with "regular members" of the Church of England.[66]

Nevertheless, the direction taken by the Reformed movement in New England inevitably gravitated toward denominational fragmentation. The most serious division came about as a result of the mid-eighteenth-century Great Awakening revival, which pitted evangelical New Lights against formalistic Old Lights. Later, at the time that the legal separation of church and state forced Congregationalists to redefine their institutional foundations, the "Unitarian Controversy" further divided the movement. At issue was the nature of the Trinity. Under the leadership of William Ellery Channing of the Federal Street Church in Boston, the Unitarian denomination gained numerous adherents, and by the 1820s many parishes openly declared their new persuasion. The pattern of religious change, begun in the seventeenth century, thus continued through to the nineteenth century, with each denomination following its own conscience while simultaneously perceiving itself as the rightful heir to the Puritan tradition.[67]

Communion Furniture

One of the most visible symbols of New England reform was the communion table. As participants in the Reformed tradition, Puritans sought to demystify the religious experience, and they followed the widespread Reformed practice of placing the table in the midst of the congregation so that all could see and hear better. Depending on the specific floor plan, it was typically placed in front of the pulpit or set partially into the center aisle between the front benches or pews.[68]

The Puritan communion table was clearly domestic in its form and decoration. It replaced the "mysterious" pre-Reformation altar (often made of stone) with a familiar table form. Puritans further strengthened this idea by excluding from it religious ornamentation or symbolism. The table made about 1700 for the First Church in Newbury, Massachusetts, by Stephen Jacques (who also built the meeting house that same year) expresses this quality (Figure 129). Its basic shape and its

65. Walker, pp. 507–516; Bushman, pp. 149–154.
66. *Plymouth Church Records*, 1:334 (12 August 1770).
67. Ahlstrom, pp. 395–397, 289.
68. For a comprehensive discussion of the arrangements and uses of interior furnishings of Anglican churches see G. W. O. Addleshaw and Frederick Etchells, *The Architectural Setting of Anglican Worship* (London: Faber & Faber, 1948).

129. *Communion table from Newbury, Mass., ca. 1700.*

69. John J. Currier, *History of Newbury, Mass., 1635–1902* (Boston: Damrell & Upham, 1902), p. 333. No mention is made of the Newbury table; its use as a communion table is based on tradition. The two long tables are owned by the Wadsworth Atheneum, Hartford, Connecticut, and are published in Wallace Nutting, *Fur-*

decorative moldings, turnings, and paint are common to many pieces of seventeenth-century household furniture. Two other seventeenth-century communion tables are known, and they also reinforce the preference for secular designs. Both are large, rectangular tables, whose privately owned counterparts appear in personal estate inventories as "great tables."[69]

A second type of table used in the seventeenth century was hinged to some stationary surface, as opposed to being freestanding. The contract for the 1658 Malden, Massachusetts, meeting house specified that the table be attached to the deacon's pew "to fall downe" when it was to be used. A similar "hanging table before the deacons' seat" was specified in Framingham, Massachusetts, in 1710.[70] In the absence of deacons' pews, these rectangular or semicircular boards may have been attached to the front of the pulpit. Hanging tables may have been necessary in some meeting houses due to space limitations. However, a lack of space implies a decision not to provide it, since great care was exercised in the interior arrangement of benches and pews. Consequently, these tables may be understood as a further removal from the idea of an altar as having sacred and mysterious qualities. They purposely did not provide a visual and symbolic focus that Puritans would have regarded as distracting. Instead, they were purely functional— when not in use, they hung out of the way and out of the mind of the congregation. Evidence suggests that toward the end of the eighteenth century hanging tables were gradually replaced by standing tables (as in Bentley's own church in 1786)[71], which seems to coincide roughly with the acceptance of the church plan and other Anglican architectural features into the Congregational mode.

The evolution of the communion table shows that the Reformed ideal of using domestic-object forms remained fixed through the early nineteenth century. The table made in 1826 by Jacob Fisher, Jr., for the First Church in Berlin, Massachusetts, is a domestic side table showing little adaptation to its specialized ecclesiastical purpose except for its slightly larger dimensions, which probably reflect its placement in a spacious architectural setting (Figure 131).

The continued use of secular forms is also apparent in deacons' benches and other meetinghouse seating furniture. The deacons' bench made for the Tabernacle Church in Salem, Massachusetts (a Congregational offspring of the First Church), is similar in its form and decoration to many other examples of Windsor furniture made for civic or household use (Figure 134). Two banister-back side chairs that survive with meetinghouse associations are indistinguishable from their domestic counterparts. The first, probably made in the 1720s or 1730s, carries an inscription stating that it was "first used in Westboro [Massachusetts] Meeting House" (Figure 132). A brass plaque on a late eighteenth-century chair owned by the Exeter, New Hampshire, Congregational Church records its previous use as a pulpit chair (Figure 133). Sometimes interior renovations of meeting houses, which often focused on the pulpit area, provided space for pulpit sofas—many of which are still in use. Finally, a Windsor armchair, made by Joseph Wilder and presented to the Acworth, New Hampshire, church about 1821, has a design (probably representing the tablet of the laws) painted on its crest rail (Figure 135).

Beginning in the 1830s and 1840s, Gothic designs, which had never

niture of the Pilgrim Century, 1620–1720, 2 vols. (1924; reprint ed., New York: Dover Publications, 1965), 2:478 (Fig. 694) and 484 (Fig. 698). See Robert F. Trent, "The Joiners and Joinery of Middlesex County, Massachusetts, 1630–1730," in Arts of the Anglo-American Community in the Seventeenth Century, ed. Ian M. G. Quimby (Charlottesville, Va.: Published for the Henry Francis DuPont Winterthur Museum by the University Press of Virginia, 1975), p. 140. Suitable examples for all references to objects in personal estate inventories cited may be found in Rural Household Inventories, 1675–1775, ed. Abbott Lowell Cummings (Boston: Society for the Preservation of New England Antiquities, 1964).

70. Bicentennial Book of Malden, p. 124; Manual of the Church of Christ, Framingham, Mass. (Boston: Wright, Potter, 1870), p. 21.

71. Bentley, Diary, 1:49 (7 January 1786).

131. Communion table purchased for the second meeting house in Berlin, Mass., 1826.

134. Deacons' bench from the Tabernacle Church, Salem, Mass. Early nineteenth century.

132. *Bannister back side chair used in the meeting house at Westborough, Mass., ca. 1720–1740.*

133. *Bannister back side chair used in the second meeting house in Exeter, N.H. Late eighteenth century.*

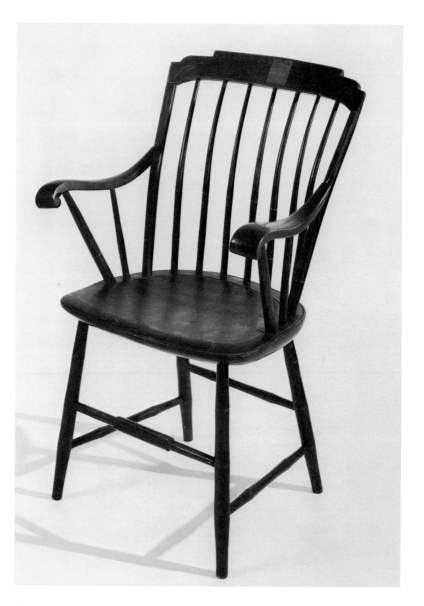

fully disappeared from use, enjoyed a marked increase in popularity. They were applied with particular emphasis to church architecture and interior furnishings, and they persisted through many subsequent changes in style and taste. An early use of Gothic revival forms (which should be distinguished from the preceding neo-Gothic designs, rep-

resented by the Federal Street pulpit, and from true medieval forms) can be seen in a deacon's chair made in 1832 for the fourth building of the First Church in Plymouth, Massachusetts, completed late in 1831 (Figure 136). Like the church building (which burned in 1892 but which is preserved in illustrations), the chair displays convention-

72. Congregational Church of Hampton, N.H., *Church Records 1731–1766*, 2:119 (5 January 1749 and 3 March 1749).

73. This information has been provided by Henry J. Harlow of Shrewsbury, Massachusetts.

alized motifs in a manner that has been termed "carpenter's Gothic," reflecting a nonacademic application of these designs.

Unlike silver and pewter communion vessels, which survive in relative abundance, most of the furniture used in New England meeting houses before the 1830s has disappeared. Only a handful of tables and chairs are known—a surprising fact given the needs of the hundreds of parishes that existed in this two-hundred-year period. The use of domestic forms partially explains the discrepancy. Undoubtedly, after new pieces of furniture were substituted for the old, the latter were pressed into domestic service, where their meetinghouse associations were easily forgotten. An additional reason for the low survival rate is that, being publicly owned, this furniture may not have benefited from the same degree of care and attention that family owned objects received.

Another type of object of which only a few examples survive is the cloth used to cover the communion table during the Lord's Supper. Puritan communion tables lacked a sense of spiritual presence, but their appearance was enhanced by the use of this important piece of church property. Although contemporary references to tablecloths are scarce, church records list them, sometimes accompanied by napkins, with the various communion vessels. The importance of these items is shown by votes of thanks directed to donors, which also appear sporadically in church records: "Some worthy Gentlewoman in Boston" gave the Congregational Church in Hampton, New Hampshire, a "Large and Beautiful Damask Table Cloth for the use of the Sacramental Table" in 1749. (The pastor noted in the records that the anonymous donor was his "Hon^d Mother, Mrs. Isabella Rand.") Two months after this gift, the church voted to divide the large cloth in two.[72]

As with the communion vessels, the deacons, and sometimes the minister, were charged with the care of the tablecloth. And like the church plate, it did not remain on the table at all times but was taken out of storage for the administration of the sacrament. Despite this care, only two early communion cloths and one napkin are known. The first is a seventeenth-century Dutch linen damask used by the church in Shrewsbury, Massachusetts, depicting the story of Caleb and Joshua returning from the Promised Land (Figure 177). It was brought from Hingham, Massachusetts, to Shrewsbury by the wife of Job Cushing, the first minister, and has a reliable *Mayflower* history.[73]

A second communion cloth and a napkin, both made of linen, were part of the "communion furniture" (which included communion vessels in the early usage of this term) of the Congregational Church in

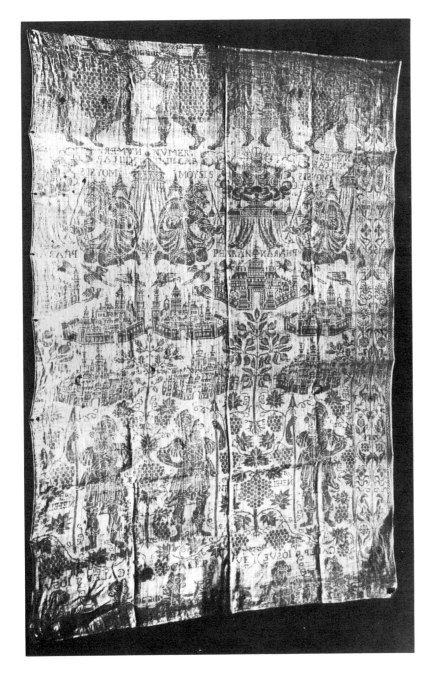

177. Photograph of linen damask communion cloth used in the church at Shrewsbury, Mass., during the eighteenth century.

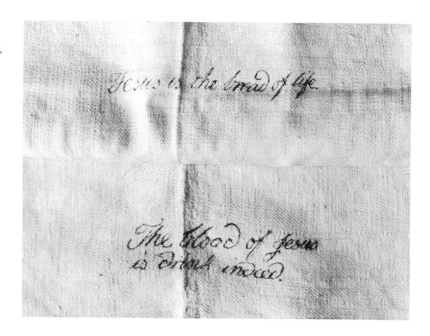

178. Detail, linen damask communion cloth and napkin used by the Congregational Church in Rockingham, Vt., in the early nineteenth century.

74. Winthrop, *Winthrop's Journal*, 1:137 (5 November 1634). The controversy was carried over into the following year.
75. George Colman, *Early Town Records* (pamphlet) (1915; reprint ed., Concord, Mass.: Concord Antiquarian Society, 1956), pp. 6–7.

Rockingham, Vermont (Figure 178). They are inscribed "The Blood of Christ is Drink indeed" and "Jesus is the Bread of Life," respectively—a distinct pronouncement of their ecclesiastical purpose. The appearance of religious inscriptions and symbols on objects or in the meeting house is not usually considered a part of the New England Congregational tradition. Seventeenth-century Boston Puritans, for example, refused to fly the British flag because it contained a cross, which was considered a "relique of antichrist."[74] However, the Rockingham cloth is not alone in this regard. A blue and white earthenware plate with the religious monogram "IHS" (*In Hoc Signo*), a cross, and three undecipherable marks descended through the Estabrook family of Concord, Massachusetts, with the tradition that it was used in the First Parish by the Reverend Joseph Estabrook (Figure 173). Although the record is unclear as to when Estabrook arrived in Concord to assist the minister, he assumed the office of pastor of the First Parish in 1694 and remained until his death in 1711.[75]

The appearance of religious motifs on some ecclesiastical objects in contrast to the strict adherence to secular designs on others underscores the fact that New England Congregationalism was not monolithic. Each gathered church was free to establish its own notions and practices of piety within limits of toleration expressed by neighboring

parishes. The result was considerable diversity throughout New England. Permissiveness, perceived as a closer imitation of the Church of England, characterized one end of the spectrum; "primitiveness" the other.

Communion Vessels

The seventeenth-century New England communion service included a wide variety of domestic forms that had been designated for church use. Among the most imposing of these forms is that represented by the silver standing cup (or chalice as it was later called) John Winthrop brought from England and gave to the First Boston Church in 1630 (Figure 138). The repoussé ornamentation covering the cup expresses secular themes and suggests that the cup was used for nonreligious purposes in the twenty years between its manufacture and its subse-

138. Silver standing cup given to the First Church in Boston, Mass., in 1630.

quent presentation to the church. The fact of domestic ownership of standing cups is also supported by their occasional appearance in seventeenth-century personal estate inventories. Here they are often identified as wine cups and are symbols of the wealth and status of their owners.

The First Church in Dorchester, Massachusetts, benefited from another gift of personally owned silver. Mrs. Elizabeth Clement, whose initials, together with her husband's, are engraved within the chased decoration on the body, gave a two-handled (or caudle) cup to that church in 1678, a gift that is recorded by an engraved inscription (Figure 140). Another inscription commemorates the subsequent presentation of this cup "by the First Church, Dorchester, to the Second Church. Jan. 1ˢᵗ 1878."

Pewter objects were also donated for the celebration of the Lord's

140. Silver two-handled cup presented in 1678 to the First Church in Dorchester, Mass.

76. New Hampshire Historical Society, Registration Files, accession number 1839.2.

159. *Pewter beaker used by the Church in Salisbury, N.H., after 1660.*

Supper. An early history accompanying a beaker states that it was brought from England in 1660 by Deacon Enoch Eaton of Salisbury, New Hampshire, and used as a communion vessel (Figure 159).[76] Sometimes objects were actually given to the church years after they

had been used regularly for communion. Under the date 6 March 1712, the records of the First Congregational Church in Salem, Massachusetts, acknowledge a gift of two large pewter flagons "which were formerly lent to yᵉ chh."[77] Flagons, often identified as made of pewter, are listed with sufficient regularity in seventeenth-century estate inventories to suggest that they were relatively popular household items at that time, though by the eighteenth century they had become rather scarce in domestic settings. In addition to the specific forms noted, tankards, mugs, numerous kinds of cups, and plates of all sizes numbered among the domestic objects commonly used at communion.

By the mid eighteenth century, and probably earlier, a practice was firmly established whereby individuals provided funds so that objects of the deacons' or their own choosing could be purchased for church use. This practice enabled two or more individuals to combine their resources and to give jointly one or more objects. A tankard belonging to the First Parish, Beverly, Massachusetts, was the gift of no fewer than six people, two men and each of their two sons, whose names or initials are inscribed on the body (Figure 151).[78] Similarly, two men each gave one of a pair of pewter beakers to the Congregational Church in Nottingham (now Hudson), New Hampshire, in 1743 (Figure 161). Thomas Hancock's gift of a pair of silver beakers to the Church of Christ in Lexington was ensured by a provision in his will that stated that twenty pounds be set aside "in case I do not give 'em in my lifetime." The beakers, engraved with the Hancock coat of arms, were given a year after his death and cost £19.13.4.[79] Early New Englanders were not reticent about recording the value of these gifts: the £4.6 price of the "present" from Josiah Bronson to his church is inscribed in plain view on the side opposite his name (Figures 155a and 155b).

Communion objects were sometimes given from one congregation to another. A silver beaker by John Edwards of Boston, for example, is inscribed "The gift of Barnstable Chh 1716" and is the property of a Congregational church in Connecticut (Figure 144). In 1711 the Barnstable Church "gave by procurement of Mr. Elisha Paine in money to [£]2-12ˢ -3ᵈ," which was then voted to "be laid out in procuring utensils for the table of the Lord." Gifts such as this were usually predicated on an existing sense of kinship between the two churches. Often, this relationship followed the removal of church members from a "parent" church to found a new society. Just three years before this gift of money, Barnstable had "dismissed" members to establish a church in Falmouth, Massachusetts.[80] A similar relationship is apparent in the late nineteenth-century gift of Mrs. Clement's cup from the First to the Second Church in Dorchester. It also accounts for a

77. *Records of the First Church in Salem* quoted in E. Alfred Jones, *The Old Silver of American Churches* (Letchworth, England: National Society of Colonial Dames of America, 1913), p. 423. This object is recorded as having been given in 1710 in a 1718 inventory of the church plate owned by this church that is reproduced in Jones, p. 424.

78. See Jones, pp. 14–15, for biographies of the donors and the circumstances of the gift.

79. Suffolk County Registry of Probate, Boston, Mass., Record Book 63: 283 (will dated 5 March 1763).

80. Jones, p. 112; Donald G. Trayser, *Barnstable: Three Centuries of a Cape Cod Town* (Hyannis, Mass.: F. B. & F. P. Gross, 1939), p. 464.

161. Pair of communion beakers given to the Church in Nottingham, N.H., in 1743.

151. Silver tankard given to the First Church in Beverly, Mass., in 1747.

155a. Silver communion beaker presented to the Church of Christ in Middlebury, Conn., in 1800.

155b. Silver communion beaker presented to the Church of Christ in Middlebury, Conn., in 1800. (reverse side of 155a).

81. Ina G. Mansur, *The Story of the First Parish in Bedford, Unitarian-Universalist* (Bedford, Mass.: First Parish in Bedford, 1967), p. 4.

contribution of six pounds from "the good people of Concord [Massachusetts] . . . for the use of the church in Bedford" in 1730.[81] Together these incidents define a pattern typical of much of the settlement of New England.

In time, as church societies and the communities they represented grew wealthier, the congregation as a whole, rather than individuals, became an important source of funds for new communion objects. The Congregational Church of Hampton, New Hampshire, for example, voted in 1744 that "ye Communion Table shall be furnished with four new [pewter] flaggons & four new Silver Cups & that ye Deacons with ye Church Committee shall endeavor to get Subscriptions for ye purchasing ye Cups & that the Pastor shall do the best he can towards

144. Silver communion beaker presented to the Church in Canterbury, Conn., by the Church in Barnstable, Mass., 1716.

purchasing both."[82] Just over eighty pounds was raised to pay for the new objects, which cost £85.7.0 (Figures 162 and 146). The new cups, by Nathaniel Hurd of Boston, matched a set of eight existing cups that had been made for the church in 1713 by John Coney, also of Boston, who had since died (Figure 145). The church voted further that "one of the old Flaggons be given to ye Pastor" and that the two remaining flagons and a tankard be sold to purchase a "Cloth for ye Sacremental Table."[83]

By the end of the eighteenth century, funds for new objects commonly came out of "the Church's stock." The First Church in Beverly, Massachusetts, drew on such a fund when it purchased a flagon from Paul Revere in 1798. A growing sense of the importance of a church's

82. Hampton, N.H., *Church Records*, 2:109 (20 February 1744).

83. Ibid., p. 112 (8 June 1744).

91

economic autonomy and well-being is reflected in the fate of the silver communion vessels once owned by the Charlestown, Massachusetts, Congregational Church. An inscription on the lid of a tankard from this church records that it was part of a service that included three large flagons given in 1703 (Figure 143). "The flaggons not being needed for Sacremental Uses were sold by Vote of the Church June 17th 1800 & the Property vested in a Town Note."

The overall demand for objects appropriate for ecclesiastical use increased markedly from the seventeenth through the nineteenth centuries as more churches came into existence and as older objects wore out. This need continued to be satisfied by both imported and domestic wares, each of which carried the stamp of its particular style period. Despite style changes in ornament, communion vessels did not reflect the introduction of new materials, forms, and uses as did the domestic objects of this two-hundred-year span. Instead, they retained seventeenth-century domestic forms that were then updated according to the prevailing style. Moreover, as the eighteenth century unfolded, the composition of communion services became more uniform until it crystallized into the distinctive communion set of the mid nineteenth century.

Throughout the period from 1700 to 1850, flagons became almost universally accepted as the container to hold the sacramental wine before it was poured into smaller vessels for distribution to the com-

*143. Silver tankard presented to the
Church in Charlestown, Mass., in 1703.*

municants. Occasionally, tankards served this purpose, though they were used for distribution as well. By about 1800 tankards began to lose favor and were replaced by either flagons or cups, depending upon how the tankards had been used. The growth in the popularity of flagons, however, was limited to their ecclesiastical role. Their domestic role was assumed by glass bottles and decanters and by ceramic and porcelain objects.

In 1724 Samuel Sewall wrote in his diary: "Deacon Checkly Deliver'd the Cup first to Madam Winthrop, and then gave me a Tankard. 'Twas humiliation to me and I think put me to the Blush to have this injustice done me by a Justice."[84] Sewall's "humiliation" suggests that the hierarchical organization of Puritan society was observed during the Lord's Supper. Presumably, those of higher social status received communion first, which parallels the concerns about "seating" the meeting house. In addition, particularly fine vessels may have been reserved for a privileged few. This public reinforcement of one's station in the community probably did not remain in practice much after Sewall's time.

By the end of the eighteenth century, uniformly shaped beakers had replaced the variety of drinking vessels in many parishes as numerous eighteenth-century pewter communion services throughout New England show. Meanwhile, the use of standing cups did not end entirely, but declined significantly. Like flagons, they were replaced in the home by more stylish glassware. William Bentley's curiosity at seeing Widow Hawthorne's "Old fashioned Silver Goblet of one pint measure" in 1790 reveals the extent to which styles and uses had changed.[85] The standing cup reemerged as the nineteenth-century goblet or chalice and became the dominant form of vessel from which communicants received the sacramental wine.

While domestic and ecclesiastical objects continued to evolve on increasingly divergent paths, occasional direct borrowings of fashionable domestic wares by churches for the communion table continued to occur. For example, a pair of wineglasses, probably made between 1730 and 1760, was reportedly used for communion in Groton, Connecticut, where an early history also cites the use of "large and dark green bottles" (Figure 174). Additionally, two "beaker glasses for the use of the church" appear in the records of the Richmond, Rhode Island, Baptist Church in 1774.[86] Perhaps the most significant introduction of an innovative domestic form was the occasional substitution of a silver bread basket like the one from North Church in Salem for the ubiquitous plate from which the sacramental bread was served (Figure 156). The 1805 date of acquisition for this object puts it at the

84. Sewall, *Diary*, 2:1023 (6 December 1724).
85. Bentley, *Diary*, 1:147 (16 February 1790).
86. Charles R. Stark, *A History of Groton, Conn., 1705–1905* (Stonington, Conn.: privately printed, 1922), p. 142; J. R. Cole, *History of Washington and Kent Counties* (New York: Preston, 1880), p. 734.

174. Pair of communion wine glasses used in the Congregational Church in Groton, Conn., in the eighteenth century.

156. Silver communion bread basket used by the North Church in Salem, Mass., after 1805.

cutting edge of this innovative form. By and large, however, these incidents are exceptions and serve primarily to mark the outward boundaries of uniformity and entrenchment in seventeenth-century domestic forms.

The formal structuring of communion objects into a set was achieved in the nineteenth century. In the early 1800s considerable attention seems to have been directed toward modernizing and otherwise altering existing communion vessels to make them more suitable. A letter pertaining to two early silver cups owned by the First Parish Unitarian Church in Beverly, Massachusetts, reveals this clearly: "As it has been thought advisable to alter some of the communion plate, shifting a handle from a cup, which had two, to a vessel which had none, I should think it very proper, if you will take the trouble, to call upon the goldsmith for his bill, & charge it among the expences of the table"[87](Figures 148 and 149). The goldsmith was Israel Trask, who later became an important pewterer.

Thereafter, churches commonly traded all or part of their composite communion services for a new set of pewter, silverplate, or silver. The metals industry responded with advertisements for sets, and in some cases, with objects that show an interchangeable use of molds. Goblets by William Calder, a Rhode Island pewterer, combine molded parts from a beaker and a nursing bottle (Figures 163, 164 and 165). Similarly, his flagon form is an adaptation of a teapot. Alternatively, some churches "renewed" their plate—"being vary Ancient, much worn, and the form of the vessels not convenient, (being chiefly Tankards)"—like the First Church in Roxbury, Massachusetts. An inventory taken after the communion plate had been melted down and reworked de-

87. This letter is reproduced and the circumstances of this alteration are discussed in Martha Gandy Fales, *Early American Silver*, rev. ed. (New York: E. P. Dutton & Co., 1973), p. 274.

163. *Pewter beaker or tumbler by William Calder, Providence, R.I., 1825–1850.*

164. *Pewter goblet or chalice by William Calder, Providence, R.I., 1825–1850.*

165. *Pewter nursing bottle by William Calder, Providence, R.I., 1825–1850.*

88. Walter Eliot Thwing, *History of the First Church in Roxbury, Massachusetts, 1630–1904* (Boston: W. A. Butterfield, 1908), pp. 256–258.
89. First Parish-Unitarian, Kennebunk, Me., *Church Records*, p. 95 (13 May 1850).

scribes the set as including nine cups with covers, one silver-plated flagon, four silver-plated plates for bread, and a tablespoon.[88]

After the First Parish–Unitarian Church in Kennebunk, Maine, had received its new silver-plated communion service, it voted in 1850 to "present the communion service recently used by this Church to the Unitarian Association of Boston to be by them presented in the name of the First Parish of Kennebunk to some destitute Parish or society."[89] In fact, the Church retained this older pewter service by Israel Trask. Obtaining communion wares for a new or poor society was always a serious problem. Most often, those churches that first used less expensive objects eventually upgraded them. Such was the case with the York Parish, Maine, which once used a wooden tankard during communion (Figure 176). Even the prominent First Church in Salem, Massachusetts, listed two "large stone jugs" among its communion wares in 1718. Sometimes, however, poor churches did not survive, like the Fifth Parish of Newbury, Massachusetts (est. 1762), for which

Daniel Bayley made an earthenware jug in 1763 (Figure 175). In 1790 Bentley observed a "deserted Meeting House once improved by a curious Mʳ Noble," who had been dismissed in 1784.[90]

Collection boxes are not directly involved in the communion ritual, but they are closely affiliated with it. Many examples from New England Congregational churches survive, most of which seem to have been made after 1800. Unfortunately, they are not mentioned in contemporary sources, and the specific circumstances of their use are somewhat uncertain. But knowledge about related factors partially fills this gap. Through the seventeenth and eighteenth centuries, towns-

176. Two wooden communion tankards used in the First Parish Church of York, Maine. Eighteenth century.

90. Jones, p. 424; Currier, p. 385; Bentley, *Diary,* 1:200 (23 September 1790). For information on Daniel Bayley see Lura Woodside Watkins, *Early New England Potters and Their Wares* (Cambridge: Harvard University Press, 1950), pp. 48–61.

people generally paid an ecclesiastical tax to support the minister and pay the operating costs of the church (though some dissenters could obtain exemptions, and the cost of communion was borne by special rates assessed to church members). As the ties between church and state were gradually severed, the need arose for another way to obtain these funds. References to collections on communion days begin to appear toward the close of the eighteenth century, and they suggest that this need was filled in a manner following the established Anglican practice of taking a collection during the offertory that came just before communion. The success of this practice is demonstrated by its continued use today, though alms basins often take the place of collection boxes.

175. Redware communion jug used in the Fifth Church in Newbury, Mass., after 1763.

Baptism

Baptism, the only sacrament besides communion to remain a part of Puritan religious practices, was performed either by total immersion or by the symbolic act of sprinkling water from a basin. (The choice of method was the prerogative of the individual congregation.) Among those churches selecting the latter, any type of basin or deep dish was suitable. Pewter and silver were the most common materials from which these basins were made, but, like communion vessels, there were no restrictions in the Reformed tradition that limited either its form or material.

In most instances early baptismal basins probably did not have a specialized stand or frame associated with them. Instead, they were most likely placed on a convenient tabletop or other horizontal surface. No evidence has been uncovered that suggests in what part of the meeting house this ceremony took place. It may have occurred near the main entrance but may also have taken place near the pulpit—symbolically in front of the entire congregation. However, the variety of practices the Reformed tradition encompassed argues that no single location can be considered typical.

The earliest of the few baptismal basin stands that have survived is a late-seventeenth-century turned stand, identifiable primarily on the basis of its form, though an accompanying history suggests that it was used in the First Church in Salem, Massachusetts (Figure 128).[91] In contrast, an eighteenth-century iron frame survives with a secure history of use in the second meeting house of the First Parish Church, Portland, Maine (Figure 179). It was probably supported by two iron rings set into the wall, one above the other. The building in which it was originally used was replaced by another in 1825–1826. Sometime later in the century, the frame was installed in this third building to the left of the pulpit in a new iron stanchion. A similar iron frame was used in Westborough, Massachusetts. There in 1739 an individual provided the money for a baptismal basin, together with "a frame for the basin, with its Shaft and Skrews, &c price 20s."[92]

Music

An integral part of the sabbath service consisted of praising God through the singing of the Psalms of David, otherwise termed the practice of psalmody. The interest of Reformed churches in psalmody is demonstrated by the fact that the first book published in New

91. Anne Farnum, "Furniture at the Essex Institute," *The Magazine Antiques* 111 (May 1977):958.
92. Letter from William B. Jordan, Jr., Church Historian, the First Parish, Portland, Maine, to Philip D. Zimmerman; Herman Packard DeForest, and Edward Craig Bates, *History of Westborough, Massachusetts* (Westborough, Mass.: privately printed, 1891), p. 91.

179. Baptismal basin frame from the second meeting house in Portland, Maine. Mid eighteenth century.

128. Baptismal stand from Salem, Mass. Seventeenth century.

England was the *Bay Psalm Book* of 1640, a new, literal translation of the Psalms by three Puritan divines. The *Bay Psalm Book* did not entirely replace earlier English psalmodies, such as Ainsworth or Sternhold and Hopkins, until the early eighteenth century (Figure 193). However, because the New England version did not contain music, many of the tunes that had been learned through English experience were forgotten or were sung in a "hideous and disorderly"

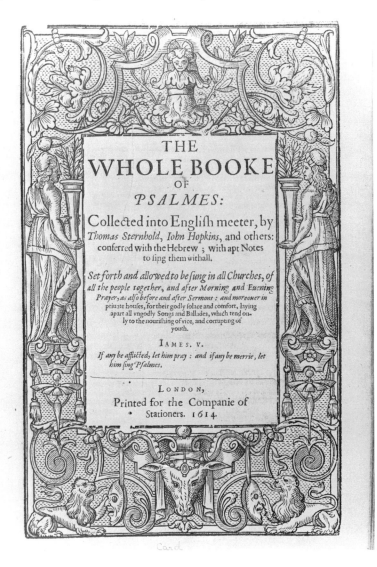

THE
WHOLE BOOKE
OF
PSALMES:

Collected into English meeter, by *Thomas Sternhold, Iohn Hopkins,* and others: conferred with the Hebrew ; with apt Notes to ſing them withall.

Set forth and allowed to be ſung in all Churches, of all the people together, and after Morning and Euening Prayer, as alſo before and after Sermons : and moreouer in priuate houſes, for their godly ſolace and comfort, laying apart all vngodly Songs and Ballades, which tend only to the nouriſhing of vice, and corrupting of youth.

Iames. v.

If any be afflicted, let him pray : and if any be merrie, let him ſing Pſalmes.

London,
Printed for the Companie of
Stationers. 1614.

193. The Whole Book of Psalmes *by Sternhold and Hopkins, 1614. Probably used in New England in the seventeenth century.*

103

93. Sewall, *Diary*, 2:885–886 (23 February 1718); 1:283 (25 October 1691).

94. *Congregational Church in Hollis, N.H.: A Brief History* (Bristol, N.H., 1893), p. 49.

manner. Sewall, who prided himself on his ability to lead religious singing, privately complained of having "set York" only to find the congregation falling into "St. Mary's" or "Hackney." He commonly set the pitch so high his own voice was unable to complete a stanza.[93]

The move to learn musical notation and to sing in parts, led by ministers in Boston, Taunton, and Bradford, Massachusetts, from 1720 to 1730 met with considerable resistance from those who had spent the better part of a lifetime singing out of tune. Innovations were regarded as "popish" and "artificial" but in the end the "new" or "regular way" of singing overcame the old way, and choristers were appointed to train singers, to teach the congregation new tunes, and to relearn old tunes accurately. New translations of the Psalms, such as Tate and Brady's *New Version of the Psalms of David* and Isaac Watts's *Psalms of David* were issued for this purpose, along with new editions of the *Bay Psalm Book* using "prickt" (perforated) notes (Figure 194).

The next step was for the trained singers to win the privilege of sitting together in a single pew or bench on the ground floor. Hollis, New Hampshire, for example, voted in 1767 to allow "those persons that have taken the pains to instruct themselves in singing [to sit in] . . . the two foreseats below on the men's side."[94] Most towns in southern New Hampshire and eastern Massachusetts allowed singers to occupy ground-floor seats in the ten-year period from 1763 to 1773. In the following decade many towns in Connecticut and central Massachusetts voted to allow singers a more commanding place in the front gallery.

Like the formation of gallery choirs, the introduction of musical accessories and instruments was accomplished only after debate and controversy. The two early nineteenth-century iron tuning forks from the Union meeting house in Salisbury, New Hampshire, were probably employed at a time when musical accessories were already an accepted feature of religious singing (Figure 192). However, the 1788 pitch pipe of Scottish origin that has a history from the Scottish-Irish town of Londonderry, New Hampshire, was presumably used by the town's chorister when accessories of this type were still controversial (Figure 190). At the same meeting in 1770 in which it outlawed the "swinging of the hand," Sterling, Massachusetts, disallowed the chorister the use of a pitch pipe. A pitch pipe was similarly disallowed in East Windsor, Connecticut, in 1780. A church vote in 1772 in Kensington, Connecticut, however, did allow a pitch pipe with the clear understanding "yt if the Choiristers modestly use what they call the Pitch Pipe it shall give . . . no offence." Again, it was the ministry

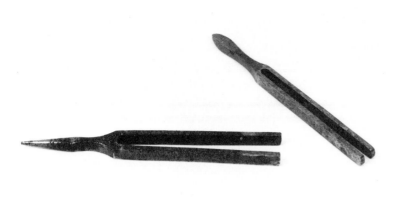

192. Two tuning forks used in the Salisbury, N.H., Union meeting house in the nineteenth century.

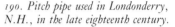

190. Pitch pipe used in Londonderry, N.H., in the late eighteenth century.

who supported the innovations. In the words of Zabdiel Adams, who delivered a lecture at Lancaster, Massachusetts, urging the adoption of regular singing, a pitch pipe "enables us to begin and set the tune at a proper height or pitch, that so the notes of it may be within the compass of different voices." The "motion of the hand," he added, allowed the congregation "to keep exact time and sing in perfect consonance."[95]

From pitch pipes and tuning forks, the proponents of musical cultivation advanced to other instruments. Waterbury, Connecticut, was using a "timbrell" (a small drum) and two "taboreans" (presumably tambourines) for the psalmody in 1792.[96] Scores of parishes introduced the bass viol in the years from 1790 to 1810, many of these instruments being fabricated by local residents. The inscribed bass viol "Laus Deo" ("Praise Be to God"), which has come down through a New Hampshire family, represents one of several sizes of viols whose introduction coincided, too, with the widespread adoption of new collections of hymns (Figure 189). By 1850 violins, flutes, violas, clarinets, and cellos had joined the bass viols; some churches soon were using melodeons and organs.

95. *150th Anniversary of Sterling, Massachusetts* (Sterling, Mass.: privately printed, 1931), p. 10; Stiles, *History of Ancient Windsor*, p. 256; *Two-Hundredth Anniversary, Kensington Congregational Church*, p. 38; Zabdiel Adams, *The Nature, Pleasure and Advantages of Church-Musick: A Sermon Preached at a Lecture in the First Parish of Lancaster, 1771* (Boston: Richard Draper, 1771), p. 36.

96. Joseph Anderson, *Town and City of Waterbury*, 3 vols. (New Haven: Price & Lee, 1896), 1:612.

189. Bass viol probably used in New Hampshire in the early nineteenth century.

Weddings and Funerals in the Meeting House

97. Bentley, *Diary*, 1:377; Sewall, *Diary*, 1:140.

Although weddings and funerals were civic ceremonies, evidence suggests that at least a part of these public observances were conducted in the meeting house. Very little is actually known about marriage ceremonies. In Samuel Sewall's lifetime they were usually performed at night and were accompanied by psalm singing and the consumption of "Cakes" and "Possett." Whether any of these ceremonies took place in local meeting houses, however, is not easy to determine. Sewall noted in 1703 that he performed the marriage ceremony of Abigail Briscow and William Palfree "at his house" (meaning at the house of the bride's father). On a visit to Salem, Massachusetts, ten years later (22 October 1713), he witnessed the marriage of Aaron Porter and Susan Sewall "at my Brother's" house. Nevertheless, the number of guests (thirteen plus "many more present") listed by Sewall, on other occasions where no location was specified, suggests that the ceremony took place in a room larger than could be provided in a private dwelling. If weddings were not commonly taking place in Congregational meeting houses in the early eighteenth century, they were probably doing so fifty or a hundred years later. The Chandler wedding tapestry, presumed to have been made in commemoration of a wedding that took place in 1765, depicts a wedding party standing before a meeting house that in part resembles the Old South in Boston or an unidentified Anglican chapel (Figure 40). Similarly, the 1804 needlework sampler by Hope Mosely illustrates a bridal couple beside the meeting house in Wethersfield, Connecticut (Figure 43).

Various written references suggest the role of the meeting house in funerals. Most to the point is an entry in Bentley's *Diary* in which he states that "the Corpse was carried to the door of the Meeting House, & with singing, there was a prayer." From there "the body was deposited in a brick grave." Other references record the pulpit's being draped in "black cloath upon which were Scutcheons" (coats of arms) and identify the meeting house as the place where funeral palls and biers were stored. Finally, numerous votes in towns throughout New England show that these societies provided the burial cloths "to putt upon the Coffin of those who are Carried to their Graves."[97]

Behind this evidence lie other factors that support this viewpoint. Foremost is that burying grounds were typically adjacent to the meeting house. (Burying grounds nearly surrounded many Anglican churches.) This physical relationship is graphically illustrated in the ink drawing of the meeting house in York, Maine, made about 1828

12. View of town center, York, Maine, ca. 1828

(Figure 12). It is also evident in the Wadsworth map of New Haven (Figure 37) and in many mourning pictures.

Finally, the meetinghouse bell also served on funeral occasions, and local codes enabled residents of each community to "read" its meaning. The First Church in Woodbury, Connecticut, directed its bell ringer in December 1798 "to toll the bell for deaths 2 strokes for a child 4 for

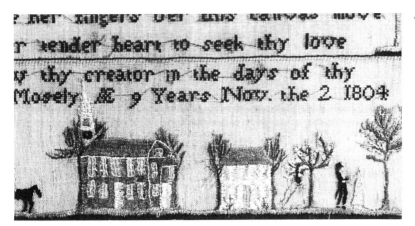

43. Detail of sampler by Hope Mosely, Wethersfield, Conn., 1804.

a woman & 6 for a man." The regulations for the ringing of the bell "for the Death of Any Person" at Centerbrook, Connecticut, on the other hand, were a little different: "For a man four Strokes for a woman three Strokes for a Male child two for a female child one the Strokes to be about the same distance from each other as when tolling for the Minister."[98]

98. Kelly, 2:320; 1:76.

Selected Bibliography

Addleshaw, G. W. O., and F. Etchells. *The Architectural Setting of Anglican Worship*. London, Faber & Faber, 1948.

Ahlstrom, Sydney, E. *A Religious History of the American People*. New Haven, Yale University Press, 1972.

Benes, Peter. "Twin-Porch *versus* Single-Porch Stairwells: Two Examples of Cluster Dispersal in Rural Meetinghouse Architecture." *Old-Time New England* 69 (Winter–Spring 1979), in press.

———, ed. *Annual Proceedings of the Dublin Seminar for New England Folklife* (1979): *New England Meeting House and Church: 1630–1850*, forthcoming.

———. "The Templeton 'Run' and the Pomfret 'Cluster': Patterns of Diffusion in Rural New England Meetinghouse Architecture, 1647–1822." *Old-Time New England* 68 (Winter–Spring 1978):1–21.

Donnelly, Marian, C. *The New England Meeting Houses of the Seventeenth Century*. Middletown, Conn., Wesleyan University Press, 1968.

Earle, Alice Morse. *The Sabbath in Puritan New England*. New York, Charles Scribner's Sons, 1891.

Fales, Martha Gandy. *Early American Silver*, rev. ed. New York, E. P. Dutton & Co., 1973.

Fennimore, Donald L. "Religion in America: Metal Objects in Service of the Ritual." *American Art Journal* 10 (November 1978): 20–42.

Foote, Henry W. *Annals of King's Chapel from the Puritan Age of New England to the Present Day*. 2 vols. Boston, Little, Brown, 1882.

Garvan, Anthony. "The Protestant Plain Style before 1630." *Journal of the Society of Architectural Historians* 9 (October 1950): 5–13.

Jones, E. Alfred. *The Old Silver of American Churches*. Letchworth, England, National Society of Colonial Dames of America, 1913.

Kelly, J. Frederick. *Early Connecticut Meetinghouses*. 2 vols. New York, Columbia University Press, 1948.

Marlowe, George Francis. *Churches of Old New England*. New York, Macmillan, 1947.

Montgomery, Charles F. *A History of American Pewter*, New York, Praeger, 1973.

Place, Charles A. "From Meeting House to Church in New England." *Old-Time New England* 13–14 (October 1922; January, April, July 1923).

Porter, Noah. "The New England Meeting House." 1882. Reprinted in *Tercentenary Commission of the State of Connecticut*, pp. 1–34. New Haven, Yale University Press, 1933.

Rose, Harold W. *The Colonial Houses of Worship in America*. New York, Hastings House, 1963.

Sinnott, Edmund M. *Meetinghouse & Church in Early New England*. New York, McGraw-Hill, 1963.

Speare, Eva. *Colonial Meetinghouses of New Hampshire*. 1938; rev. ed. Littleton, N.H.: Reginald M. Colby, Agent, 1955.

Walker, Williston. *The Creeds and Platforms of Congregationalism*. 1893. Reprint. Boston, Pilgrim Press, 1960.

Wight, Charles A. *Some Old-Time Meeting Houses of the Connecticut Valley*. Chicopee Falls, Mass., Rich Print, 1911.

Winslow, Ola E. *Meeting House Hill, 1630–1783*. New York, Macmillan, 1952.

Catalogue of the Exhibition

Dimensions are to the nearest ⅛ inch, and reflect overall measurements. Most materials have been identified by visual examination only.

Architectural paintings, drawings, prints, and maps

1
TOWNSCAPE
"The Second Meeting House, South Hadley"
Joseph Goodhue Chandler, 1813–1884
South Hadley, Mass., early nineteenth century
Oil on wood; H. 12½ in., w. 15½ in.
Signed in lower left: "J. G. Chandler"
Shows the second meeting house (1761–1844) in South Hadley, Mass., after the bell tower was added in 1791 and after the interior was "turned," eliminating the long-side entry.
Mount Holyoke College Art Museum, South Hadley, Mass.

1

3

2

TOWNSCAPE
"View of New Haven Green in
1800"
William Giles Munson, 1801–
1878
New Haven, Conn., ca. 1830
Oil on canvas; H. 30¼ in.,
w. 44¼ in.
Illustrates the use of round-
topped "Anglican" windows in an
urban Congregational meeting
house built in 1757.
New Haven Colony Historical
Society, New Haven, Conn.

3

TOWNSCAPE
"Framingham Common"
Framingham, Mass., ca. 1840
Oil on canvas; H. 15 in.,
w. 22 in. (sight)
Said to be a copy by a General

Gordon, probably George H.
Gordon (1823–1886) of Framingham, of a picture of Framingham Common made by Dan-
iel Bell in 1808; the original is now
lost. The white meeting house
standing in the distance behind
Abner Wheeler's tavern was the
third building of the First Parish
in Framingham, built in 1807 and
torn down in 1830.
Private collection

4

PEW DOOR
New Hampshire, mid-eighteenth
century
Pine; polychrome; H. 37¾ in.,
w. 20½ in.
"NEW PARISH / MEETING HOUSE.
/ EXETER, N.H. / 1741–1823"
painted on lower panel, probably
in the nineteenth century.

Shows the first meeting house
(1743) of the Second Congregational Church in Exeter, painted
in grays and white.
First Parish Church in Exeter,
N.H.

5

ARCHITECTURAL DRAWING
Concord, Mass., 1841
Pencil and oil on pine board;
H. 16⅞ in., w. 18⅛ in.
"Built 1712 by Charles Underhill
/ Enlarged & repaired 1791 by
Abner Wheeler / Remodled 1841
by Nathan S. Hosmer"; "Built
1712, ENLARGED & REPAIRED
1791, REMODELLED 1841"; and
"Outlines of the old unitarian
house Concord, taken June the
15th 1841 by W" inscribed in pen-
cil on front; similar inscriptions
on back.
Meeting house painted yellow.
Drawing possibly by John R.
Wesson, who also made a model
of the Concord meeting house
(Catalogue no. 69).
Museum of the Concord Anti-
quarian Society, Concord, Mass.
M-407

6

ARCHITECTURAL LANDSCAPE
"Ye Old South Meetin House
1763"
Worcester, Mass., ca. 1887
Oil on cedar shingle;
H. 15⅝ in., w. 4 in.
Painted on a shingle from the
church, which was torn down in
1887.
Worcester Historical Museum,
Worcester, Mass. 1948.62

4

5

6

7

8

Signed in lower right: "M. E. Dickson"
Donated by the artist in 1889.
Worcester Historical Museum, Worcester, Mass. 1978.1078

9
THREE ARCHITECTURAL DRAWINGS
Plymouth, Mass., late eighteenth century
Ink on paper; top, H. 3½ in., w. 5 in.; bottom, H. 3¼ in., w. 4⅜ in.
"Meeting Hous Plymouth Built 1683" on top front; "Built in the year 1683. Taken down 1744 / 45 feet by 40 — 16 in the walls. Scale / 20 feet to an inch. It stood where / the first Church now stands. / MEETING HOUSE" on bottom front; "1744 / 71 feet & ten inches in front and / 67 feet 8 inches deep [?] / Its spire 100 feet high was / surmounted by a brass weather-cock" on top back.

7
ARCHITECTURAL LANDSCAPE
"Old South Church. 1763–1887"
Worcester, Mass., ca. 1887
Oil on pine architectural fragment; H. 7 in., w. 3¼ in.
Worcester Historical Museum, Worcester, Mass. 1978.1079

8
ARCHITECTURAL LANDSCAPE
"Old South Meeting House 1763"
Mabel E. Dickson
Worcester, Mass., ca. 1887
Oil on slate; H. 20¾ in., w. 18 in.

Possibly drawn by Samuel Davis (1765–1829).
Pilgrim Society, Plymouth, Mass.

10
MANUSCRIPT JOURNAL
Dudley Woodbridge, 1705–1790
Deerfield, Mass., 1728
"Delineated at Deerfield" and "Deerfield Meeting Houses" inscribed in margin. Page three of a four-page journal kept by Dudley Woodbridge from October 1 to 10, 1728, while on a trip through the Connecticut Valley. A physician, minister, and merchant, Woodbridge resided in Stonington, Conn.
Shows a pen-and-ink illustration of the second meeting house in Deerfield, erected 1694 and taken down 1729. Two larger meeting houses, possibly those at Springfield and West Springfield, Mass., are shown on the same page.
Massachusetts Historical Society, Boston, Mass.

11
ARCHITECTURAL LANDSCAPE
Hopkinton, N.H., 1826
Ink on paper; H. 5 in., w. 4½ in.
"Congregational Meeting-House / Hopkinton N.H. / 1826" inscribed on bottom.
The building, which still survives, replaced an earlier meeting house around 1789. The central pavilion was added about 1800; the tower was erected between 1809 and 1811.
New Hampshire Historical Society, Concord, N.H. 1971.51

9b

old Congregational church, court-house, Captain Wilcox's tavern, and old cemetery.

The church has since been rotated 90 degrees to face the road that now separates it from the burying ground.

Old Gaol Museum, York, Me. 1977·77

13

13

ARCHITECTURAL LANDSCAPE
"The Fourth Edifice, 1749–1846"
Roxbury, Mass., 1847
Pencil on paper;
H. 6¾ in., w. 9⅛ in. (sight)
"Roxbury Jan 1847" and "A. D. Bugbee" inscribed in lower left and right respectively.

Shows the fourth building of the First Church in Ipswich, Mass. Samuel C. Bugbee, presumed to be a relative of A. D. Bugbee's, was the architect of the fifth building, which was destroyed by fire in 1965.

First Church in Ipswich, Mass.

12
TOWNSCAPE
D. B. Harris
York, Maine, ca. 1828
Ink on paper; H. 14 in.,
w. 20 in.
"Pen sketch by D. B. Harris many years ago" inscribed in lower right. Buildings identified as old Congregational parsonage,

117

16

14

TOWNSCAPE
Maria E. Perry, 1826–1849
Dublin, N.H., ca. 1846–1849
Pencil on paper; H. 14 in.,
W. 18 in.
Illustrates the 1818 Dublin meet-
ing house on top of the hill and
the brick First Trinitarian
Church, erected in 1836.
New Hampshire Historical Soci-
ety, Concord, N.H. 1943.4

15

ARCHITECTURAL LANDSCAPE
"View of the Old Brick Meeting
House in Boston 1808."
James Kidder
Boston, early nineteenth century
Aquatint; H. 4½ in., W. 6⅛ in.
"Drawn by I. R. Smith" in lower
left; "Engraved by J. Kidder" in
lower right.
Old Brick, the third meeting
house of the First Church in Bos-
ton, stood from 1712 to 1808.
Massachusetts Historical Society,
Boston, Mass.

16

ARCHITECTURAL LANDSCAPE
"East Church, Salem. Built 1718"
Bufford & Co., Boston, Mass.,
ca. 1847
Lithograph; H. 8⅛ in., W. 5½ in.
(image)
Original drawn by D. M. She-
pard. Issued with interior view
(Catalogue no. 17).
Essex Institute, Salem, Mass.
120,087.1

17

17
INTERIOR VIEW
"Interior of East Church, Salem"
Bufford & Co., Boston, Mass.,
ca. 1847
Lithograph; H. 5¾ in., w. 8¼ in.
(image)
Original drawn by D. M. She-
pard. Issued with exterior view
(Catalogue no. 16). Shows box
pews and stovepipes.
Essex Institute, Salem, Mass.
103,116K

18
ARCHITECTURAL LANDSCAPE
"Trinity Church, Newport,
R.I."
Robertson, Seibery & Shearman,
New York, ca. 1860
Lithograph; H. 11⅞ in.,
w. 9½ in. (image)
Original drawn by J. P. Newell.
Illustrates the second building of
Trinity Church, Newport, R.I.,

erected in 1726.
American Antiquarian Society,
Worcester, Mass.

19
ARCHITECTURAL LANDSCAPE
"View of Old Trinity Church."
Probably Massachusetts, ca. 1834
Woodcut; H. 3 in., w. 3 in.
Published in *The American Maga-
zine of Useful and Entertaining
Knowledge*, vol. 1, no. 1 (1834),
p. 18.
The first building of Trinity
Church, Boston, erected in 1735.
American Antiquarian Society,
Worcester, Mass.

20
TOWNSCAPE
"The Battle of Lexington. April
19ᵗʰ 1775. Plate I."
Amos Doolittle, 1754–1832
New Haven, Conn., 1775
Hand-colored line engraving;

H. 11¾ in., w. 17⅜ in. (image)
"A. Doolittle, Sculpᵗ" in lower
right.
Copy of a painting by Ralph
Earle.
Essex Institute, Salem, Mass.
115,513

21
ARCHITECTURAL DESIGN BOOK
James Gibbs
*Book of Architecture containing
designs of buildings & ornaments*
(London, 1728), 150 plates
A second copy of this book, now
at the Boston Athenaeum, has
"Providence" inscribed in pencil
above the middle spire on Plate
30. It was owned by Thomas
Dawes, architect of the Brattle
Square Church.
Providence Athenaeum, Provi-
dence, R.I.

22
ARCHITECTURAL LANDSCAPE
"North West View of
Charlestown Meeting House"
E. W. Bouve, Boston, Mass.,
1846
Lithograph; H. 10⅞ in.,
w. 8⅞ in. (image)
From a 1799 drawing published
in Richard Frothingham's *History
of Charlestown*, 1846.
Shows the 1783 meeting house
with its steeple designed by
Charles Bulfinch and built by
Captain D. Goodwin, Jr.
American Antiquarian Society,
Worcester, Mass.

22

23

24

23
ARCHITECTURAL LANDSCAPE
"West Church, Lynde Street, Boston"
Probably Massachusetts, mid-nineteenth century
Relief print; H. 10 in., w. 8 in.
Signed in lower right: "Schenck"
From an illustrated magazine.
120

Shows the second meeting house of the West Church in Boston, designed by Asher Benjamin, 1806.
American Antiquarian Society, Worcester, Mass.

24
ARCHITECTURAL LANDSCAPE
"Fourth House of Worship, Chauncy Place, 1808"
Probably Massachusetts, mid-nineteenth century
Relief print; H. 9 in., w. 6 in.
Removed frontispiece of a book.
Shows the fourth meeting house of the First Church in Boston.
American Antiquarian Society, Worcester, Mass.

25

25
PLATE
Clews Potteries, active ca. 1818–1834
Staffordshire, England, ca. 1830
Hard white ware, transfer printed in blue; DIAM. 8¾ in.
"CLEWS WARRANTED STAFFORD-SHIRE" with crown impressed in bottom; "WINTER VIEW OF PITTS-FIELD MASS / CLEWS" with eagle printed on bottom.
Shows the front elevation of the Pittsfield meeting house, designed by Charles Bulfinch in 1792. The building was partially destroyed by fire in 1851 and was sold by the church.
Private collection

26
ARCHITECTURAL LANDSCAPE
"Old South Church, 1763"
C. F. Jewett Co., Boston, nineteenth century
Engraved print; H. 10⅝ in., W. 7 in.
From *Heart of the Commonwealth,*

Illustrated Business Guide to the City of Worcester (Worcester, 1881), p. 69.
Illustrates the second meeting house of the First Church in Worcester, Mass., as it appeared in 1763.
American Antiquarian Society, Worcester, Mass.

27   26
ARCHITECTURAL LANDSCAPE
"Old South Church, in Worcester, As it appeared in 1776."
New England, nineteenth century
Relief print; H. 11 in., W. 8 in.
Illustrates the second meeting house of the First Church in Worcester, Mass., as it appeared in 1776.
American Antiquarian Society, Worcester, Mass.

28
ARCHITECTURAL DRAWING
"Old South Church in Worcester as it was in 1817"
William White Smith, 1882
Ink drawing on paper; H. 11⅞ in., W. 9½ in.
"Sketched by William White Smith, October 1882" inscribed on bottom.
Illustrates the second meeting house of the First Church in Worcester, Mass., as it appeared in 1817.
American Antiquarian Society, Worcester, Mass.

29
ARCHITECTURAL LANDSCAPE
"Old South Church and City Hall (1828)."
New England, ca. 1863
Engraved print; H. 5¾ in., W. 7½ in.
Frontispiece from Ira M. Barton, *Historical Discourse delivered at Worcester in the Old South Meeting House, Sept. 22, 1863* (Worcester, 1863).
Illustrates the second meeting house of the First Church in Worcester, built 1763, after the removal of the principal entry on the side and the relocation of the pulpit to the short side opposite the tower in 1828.
American Antiquarian Society, Worcester, Mass.

27

30

30
ARCHITECTURAL LANDSCAPE
New England, mid-nineteenth
century
Halftone print; H. 3½ in.,
w. 4¾ in.
Illustrates the second meeting
house of the First Church in
Worcester, built 1763, after being
"turned" in 1828.
American Antiquarian Society,
Worcester, Mass.

31
EXTERIOR VIEW
Worcester, Mass., late
nineteenth century
Photograph; H. 8½ in.,
w. 4¼ in.
Illustrates the second meeting
house of the First Church in
Worcester after the windows were
altered in 1871 to conform to the
prevailing style.
American Antiquarian Society,
Worcester, Mass.

32
INTERIOR VIEW
Worcester, Mass., late
nineteenth century
Photograph; H. 7½ in.,
w. 9⅛ in.
Illustrates the interior of the sec-
ond meeting house of the First
Church in Worcester after altera-
tions were made in 1871.
American Antiquarian Society,
Worcester, Mass.

33
EXTERIOR VIEW
Worcester, Mass., 1887
Photograph; H. 7⅜ in.,
w. 8⅝ in.
Illustrates the second meeting
house of the First Church in
Worcester at the beginning of the
building's demolition in 1887.
American Antiquarian Society,
Worcester, Mass.

34
EXTERIOR VIEW
Worcester, Mass. 1887
Photograph; H. 4¾ in.,
w. 6¾ in.
Illustrates the second meeting
house of the First Church in
Worcester being taken down in
1887.
American Antiquarian Society,
Worcester, Mass.

35
EXTERIOR VIEW
Worcester, Mass., 1887
Blueprint photograph; H. 6⅜ in.,
w. 4 in.
Illustrates the second meeting
house of the First Church in
Worcester being taken down in
1887.
American Antiquarian Society,
Worcester, Mass.

32

33

34

35

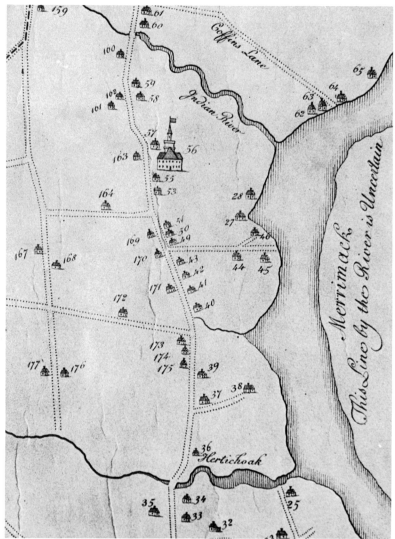

36

124

36

MAP

"A Plan of the West Parish or Newbury new Town"

Tappan & Bradford's, Lithographers

Boston, Mass., 1806

Lithograph; H. 26⅛ in., w. 22 in.

Lithograph of "A Plan of the West Parish or Newbury new Town Taken Septʳ 15 1729 by John Brown Survrʳ" which was prepared to support the petition of the parish to separate from Newbury, Mass. West Parish was set off as the Fourth Parish in 1731. Historical Society of Old Newbury, Newbury, Mass.

37

MAP

"A Plan of the Town of New Haven, With all the Buildings in 1748"

Thomas Kensett, 1786–1829

New Haven, Conn., 1806

Hand-colored copperplate engraving; H. 27 in., w. 19 ½ in.

Copy of an original by General James Wadsworth (1730–1817) of Durham, Conn., now in the collection of Yale University.

New Haven Colony Historical Society, New Haven, Conn.

38

TOWNSCAPE

"Town of Rindge, New Hampshire"

Mary Parker Kimball, 1809–ca. 1842

Rindge, N.H., before 1839

Ink and watercolor on paper; H. 12¾ in., w. 15⅝ in. (sight)

"Painted by Mary Kimball" inscribed on back of frame.

Shows the 1796 Rindge meeting house before it was altered in 1839. Ingalls Memorial Library, Rindge, N.H.

Loaned by the Wellington Family Heirs, Courtesy of the Rindge Historical Society

Embroidery and mourning pictures

39

EMBROIDERED SAMPLER

Attributed to Mary Whitehead

Middletown, Conn., ca. 1750

Wool on canvas; H. 17½ in., w. 21½ in. (sight)

"MW" in top center.

Shows blue meeting house or courthouse.

Lyman Allyn Museum, New London, Conn. 1974.94

40

FRAGMENT FROM EMBROIDERED PICTURE

Probably Massachusetts, ca. 1756

Silk and wool on linen; H. 20½ in., w. 14¾ in. (sight)

"1756" on bell tower.

Originally owned by Mrs. Hannah (Greene) Chandler, who married Gardiner Chandler in 1755. American Antiquarian Society, Worcester, Mass.

41

EMBROIDERED SAMPLER

Susan Smith, 1783–?

Rhode Island, 1793–1794

Silk on canvas; H. 16¾ in., w. 16¾ in. (sight)

Inscriptions: "Let Virture be A Guide to thee"; "Octʳ. 29. 17 93."; "Susan Smith / Was born May 28 1783 and / Wrought this May 9 1794"; "In thy fair Book of life divine My God inscribe this Name / There let it fill some humble Place Beneath the slaughter'd Lamb"

Shows the First Baptist Church, built in 1775, in considerable detail.

The Henry Francis du Pont Winterthur Museum, Winterthur, Del. 58.2879

42

EMBROIDERED PICTURE

Bia Hale, 1792–1874

Alstead, N.H., ca. 1802

Silk on linen; H. 7½ in., w. 6⅛ in. (sight)

Illustrates the 1802 Baptist meeting house in Alstead, N.H.

Thread colors: window and doors, light blue; cornice, yellow; clapboards and tower, light beige; roof, beige-pink.

Daughters of the American Revolution Museum, Washington, D.C., Gift of Miss Maybelle Still

44

with a reddish roof.
The Webb-Deane-Stevens
Museum, Wethersfield, Conn.
1946c 2 s 14

46
MOURNING PICTURE
New England, ca. 1812
Watercolor on paper;
H. 18 in., w. 19¾ in. (sight)
"In memory / of Mr. Joseph Joy
/ born Sep^t 29, 1784 / died June
12, 1812 / Aged 27 years"
inscribed on tomb.
Shows green meeting house in
background.
Gore Place, Waltham, Mass.

47
MOURNING PICTURE
Hannah Punderson, ca. 1777–
1821
Preston, Conn., ca. 1820–1825
Ink and watercolor on paper;
H. 16½ in., w. 20⅜ in. (sight)
Picture completed after Hannah's
death. House of worship in the
background is painted an off-
white color.
Connecticut Historical Society,
Hartford, Conn. 1964.40.1

48
MOURNING PICTURE
New England, early nineteenth
century
Ink and watercolor on paper;
H. 15¼ in., w. 17⅞ in. (sight)
"IN MEMORY OF / Mr CYRUS COLE
WHO DEPAR / TED THIS LIFE
MARCH 4th 1814 / IN THE 22^d
YEAR OF HIS / AGE" inscribed on

43
EMBROIDERED SAMPLER
Hope Mosely, 1795–1806
Wethersfield, Conn., 1804
Silk and wool on linen;
H. 11¾ in., w. 15 in. (sight)
Inscription: "Sampler
embroidered by H.M., age 9,
Nov. 2, 1804"
Eleanor B. Wolf

44
EMBROIDERED SAMPLER
Sarah F. Sweet, 1806–1831
Rhode Island, ca. 1820
Silk and wool on canvas;
H. 10½ in., w. 9 in.
126

Inscriptions: "The first Congregational Church / in Providence
was / destroyed by fire / June 14th
1814"; "Sarah F. Sweet"
This was the second building of
the Congregational Church in
Providence, erected in 1795.
Rhode Island Historical Society,
Providence, R.I. 1968.6.13

45
MOURNING PICTURE
Lucy Griswold, 1790–?
Springfield, Mass., ca. 1805
Silk on linen; H. 14¾ in.,
w. 12¾ in.
Illustrates a tan meeting house

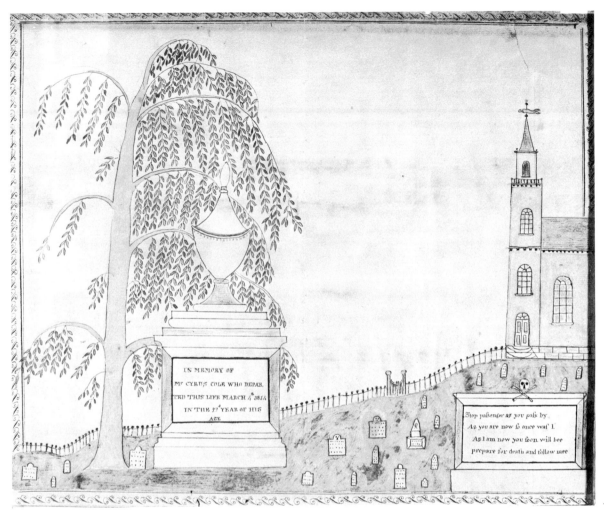

left stone; "Stop passenger as you
pass by / As you are now so once
was I / As I am now you soon
will bee / prepare for death and
follow mee" inscribed on right
stone.
Illustrates a light-yellow meeting
house.
Fruitlands Museum, Harvard,
Mass.

Weather vanes and architectural fragments

49
WEATHER VANE
New England, ca. 1673
Iron, finial of unidentified metal;
painted black and gold;
H. 76½ in. (flag, 14 × 14 in.)

"1673" pierced in flag
Erected in 1673 on the cupola of
the second meeting house in Concord, Mass., completed 1672.
The building was converted to a
courthouse in 1712, and diarist
William Bentley of Salem noted
the vane on the Concord court-
house on May 26, 1790.
Private collection

49

50   *50*

WEATHER VANE
New England, ca. 1682
Iron; painted black;
H. 7 in., W. 15 in.
"1682" pierced in flag
From "Old Tunnel" Church
(1682–1827), the second meeting
house in Lynn, Mass.
Essex Institute, Salem, Mass.
2177

51
WEATHER VANE WITH STAFF
Probably Massachusetts, ca.
1688
Iron, copper; painted dark gray;
H. 72 in. (flag, 10 × 15⅛ in.)
"1688" pierced in flag
From the second meeting house
(1663–1748) in Wenham, Mass.
Wenham Historical Association
and Museum, Wenham, Mass.

52
WEATHER VANE AND POLE
Massachusetts or England, ca.
1763
Copper, iron pole; gilded;
rooster; H. 53 in., W. 41 in.,
D. 6½ in.; pole: L. 12 ft.
From the spire of the second
meeting house of the First Church
in Worcester, Mass. (1763–1887),
also known as the Old South
Church.
Worcester Historical Museum,
Worcester, Mass. 1931.9

53
WEATHER VANE
Massachusetts, late eighteenth
century
Iron; painted gold;
H. 16½ in., W. 77½ in., D. 3 in.
From the fourth meeting house
of the First Parish in Dorchester
(1744–1817).
First Parish Church in
Dorchester, Mass.

52

54

54

WEATHER VANE
Probably Massachusetts, ca.
1823
Copper; gilded; H. 63 in.,
W. 74 in., D. 2¼ in.
From the Second Parish Church
(Old Central) in Worcester,
Mass., erected in 1823.
Worcester Historical Museum,
Worcester, Mass. 1887.28

55

LOCK
America or England, eighteenth
century
Iron; painted black; L. 11⅛ in.,
W. 7 in., D. 3 in.
"This Lock was Taken from the
/ OLD TUNNEL Meeting House /
Errected at West Lynn Mass. /
A.D. 1682" painted on lock.
Lynn Historical Society, Lynn,
Mass.

56

BELL
Bronze; painted green; H. 18 in.,
DIAM. 18 in.
"SI DEVS PRONOBUS QUIS
CONTRA NOS — 1675" cast into
bell in relief.
Used in the second (1703)
meeting house in Sandwich,
Mass.
First Church of Christ in
Sandwich, Mass.

55

57

TWO CASEMENT WINDOWS
Massachusetts, late seventeenth
century
Pine, lead, glass;
H. 21¼ in., W. 19¼ in. each.
From Old Ship Meeting House,
Hingham, Mass., built in 1681.
Private collection

58

ROUNDED WINDOW CAP
Marblehead, Mass., 1714
Pine; painted gray with white
tracery; H. 17¼ in., W. 45 in.
D. 2 in.
One of two that were recovered
during recent architectural resto-
ration of St. Michael's Church in
Marblehead.
St. Michael's Church Archives,
Marblehead, Mass.

59

CORNICE, WINDOW FRAME, AND
SASH
Shrewsbury, Mass., ca. 1766
Pine, glass; painted white;
H. 85½ in., W. 64 in., D. 8 in.
Originally from one of three
porches of the 1766 Shrewsbury
meeting house.
Henry J. Harlow

60

DENTIL FROM WINDOW CORNICE
Shrewsbury, Mass., ca. 1766
Pine; lowest layer painted ocher;
Munsell Code 10YR 5/6;
H. 2½ in., L. 3 in., W. 2½ in.
The paint color of this fragment
from a window cornice (Catalogue
no. 59) was analyzed by the Con-
sulting Services Group of the So-
ciety for the Preservation of New
England Antiquities.
Henry J. Harlow

59

61

PULPIT WINDOW CASING
Lempster, N.H., ca. 1795
Pine; painted light greenish-gray
over light blue; H. 88 in.,
W. 39 in., D. 7⅜ in.
From the pulpit window of the
first meeting house in Lempster,
N.H., built 1794. The casing was
notched in the nineteenth century
to allow for the installation of a
second floor in the meeting house.
It was removed for repairs in
1979.
Lempster Historical Society,
Lempster, N.H.

62

DOOR
Shrewsbury, Mass., ca. 1766
Pine, iron hinges; painted gray
over darker gray on exterior
surface of door; H. 89½ in.,
W. 23¾ in.
From the 1766 Shrewsbury meet-
ing house. Originally half of a
double front door the inside sur-
face of which was unpainted.
Shrewsbury Historical Society,
Shrewsbury, Mass.

63

INTERIOR WOOD FRAGMENT
Providence, R.I., 1775
Pine; painted grayish-green;
L. 7¾ in., W. ½ in., D. ½ in.
Shows original paint color of the
interior of the First Baptist
Church in America, built in 1775.
First Baptist Church in America,
Providence, R.I.

62

64

64

STEEPLE FINIAL
Groton, Mass., late eighteenth
century
Pine and lead sheeting;
H. 29 in., DIAM. (top) 22 in.
"Charles Dickson 1826" inscribed
in the lead sheeting covering the
top.
Traces of yellow paint under
more recent white paint. From
the fourth meeting house of Groton, erected 1755. Replaced in
1972 during steeple repair work.
First Parish Unitarian, Groton,
Mass.

65

Conn., ca. 1786
Iron, brass, oak frame;
H. 25 in., W. 27⅛ in., D. 31½ in.
From the 1786 belfry of the Suf-
field meeting house (1749), which
was torn down in 1836.
Connecticut Historical Society,
Hartford, Conn. 1962.78.1

67
CLOCK WEIGHT
Connecticut, early nineteenth
century
Red sandstone; H. 29¾ in.,
W. 15⅞ in.
"This / Monument / is erecte^d in
/ Memory of the / Great Flood /
on March 21st / A D 1801 / The
he[ight] . . ." inscribed on face.
Made from a broken flood-height
marker and used in the First
Church in Windsor, Conn., from
about 1844 to 1880.
First Church in Windsor, Conn.

65
CLOCK HANDS
Massachusetts, ca. 1812
Unidentified wood, iron; gilt on
front surface, white paint on
back; minute hand: L. 76 in.,
W. 7⅛ in.; hour hand:
L. 54⅜ in., W. 7¼ in.
Installed on the First Church in

Northampton, built by Isaac
Damon in 1812.
Northampton Historical Society,
Northampton, Mass.

66
CLOCK MECHANISM
Daniel Burnap, 1759–1838
East Windsor and Coventry,

Models

68
MODEL
Rhode Island, late nineteenth century
Pine, paper, brass finial;
H. 17⅝ in., L. 15 in., W. 9 in.
Model of St. Paul's Church, Narragansett, R.I., built in 1707.
Model was presented to the Rhode Island Historical Society in 1890 by the Right Reverend Thomas M. Clark, Episcopal Bishop of Rhode Island, 1854–1903.
Rhode Island Historical Society, Providence, R.I. 1978.25.1

69
MODEL
John R. Wesson, ?–1894
Concord, Mass., 1841
Pine; painted yellow;
H. 11½ in., L. 7½ in., W. 5⅛ in.
Model of the fourth meeting house in Concord, Mass. (1712–1841).
Museum of the Concord Antiquarian Society, Concord, Mass. M-408

70

70
MODEL
Warren Day Blake
Brooklyn, Conn., 1870
Pine; painted beige;
H. 20 in., L. 15 in., W. 7¾ in.
Model of the 1771 meeting house in Brooklyn, Conn.; made from a roof shingle.
Connecticut Historical Society, Hartford, Conn. 14.1957.1

71
MODEL
Salem, Mass., nineteenth century
Unidentified wood; painted gray and white; H. 56 in., L. 31½ in., W. 23 in.
Model of the meeting house of the South Parish in Salem, also known as the Tabernacle Church, erected 1803 by architect Samuel McIntire.
Essex Institute, Salem, Mass.

71

Pulpits and pulpit fragments

72
TWO CARVED PANELS
John Houghton, 1624–1684
Dedham, Mass., 1655
Oak; diamond panel: H. 12 in.,
W. 8 in.; rectangular panel:
H. 6⅝ in., W. 14 in.
Decorative insets from the pulpit
installed in the first meeting house
in Medfield, Mass., and preserved
when the meeting house was
taken down in 1708. Traces remain of verdigris coloring which
has powdered off. The diamond-
shaped panel is attached to a fragment of eighteenth-century wain-
scoting.
Medfield Historical Society,
Medfield, Mass.

73
PULPIT FRONT
East Haven, Conn., ca. 1719
Oak; H. 33⅛ in., W. 29½ in.,
D. 9 in.
Used in the first meeting house
(1719–ca. 1768) in East Haven.
New Haven Colony Historical
Society, New Haven, Conn.

74
PULPIT AND SOUNDING BOARD
Abraham Knowlton, d. 1749?
Ipswich, Mass., 1749
Pine; painted mahogany grain.
Pulpit:
H. 80 in., W. 96 in., D. 30 in.;

sounding board: H. 18 in.,
W. 120 in., D. 60 in.
The pulpit and sounding board
may have been completed by
Abraham Knowlton's son.
First Church in Ipswich, Mass.

75
PULPIT BASE
Southington, Conn., ca. 1757
Unidentified wood; painted
yellowish-brown; H. 22¾ in.,
W. 28¾ in., D. 14¾ in.
Shell is made in three pieces ap-
plied to a solid core. From the
second meeting house in South-
ington, erected 1751 and torn
down 1828.
Barnes Museum, Southington,
Conn.

76
PULPIT FRONT
Attributed to William Crafts,
1736–1800
Boston, Mass., 1772
Mahogany with mahogany
veneer; H. 82 in., W. 46¾ in.,
D. 16⅞ in.
Two fragments from the 1772
pulpit paid for by Boston merchant John Hancock.
The Society for the Preservation
of New England Antiquities, Boston, Mass. top, 6.1960; base,
1975.195

77
PULPIT
Boston, Mass., 1809
Mahogany and mahogany veneer,
iron fittings, folding kneeling

cushion upholstered in horsehair;
H. 54 in., W. 78 in., D. 20 in.
Brass plaque: "CHANNING'S PUL-
PIT / THE DESK OF THE / HIGH
PULPIT IN THE / FEDERAL STREET
CHURCH / 1809–1860"
Accompanied by a pulpit cushion
upholstered in red silk damask.
Arlington Street Church, Boston,
Mass.

78
THREE STAIR BALUSTERS
Massachusetts, 1750–1800
Maple; stripped of paint; left:
H. 30½ in., DIAM. 1½ in.;
middle: H. 29 in., DIAM. 1½ in.;
right: H. 28⅝ in., DIAM. 1½ in.
Probably from the fourth meeting
house (1749–1846) of the First
Church in Ipswich, where they
may have been used on stairs as-
cending to the pulpit.
First Church in Ipswich, Mass.

79
STAIR BALUSTER
Beverly, Mass., ca. 1785
Maple; painted gray-white;
L. 34 in., DIAM. 1½ in.
From Old South Church, Bev-
erly, built in 1785. Baluster was
removed in 1835 and presented to
the Essex Institute in 1882.
Essex Institute, Salem, Mass.
2,085

80
FINIAL
Dorchester, Mass., mid-
eighteenth century
Maple; painted gray;

H. 12½ in., DIAM. 3⅛ in.
Probably from the fourth meeting house in Dorchester, erected 1743.
Private collection

78

81

FINIAL

Pine; painted gold and red with blue base; H. 17 in., DIAM. 10 in.

Originally surmounted the sounding board in the fourth meeting house in Concord, Mass., and was removed in 1841 when the building was remodeled.

Museum of the Concord Antiquarian Society, Concord, Mass. M-900

82

FINIAL

Massachusetts, late eighteenth century

Pine, tin; painted green and gold in 1955; H. 18½ in., DIAM. (cone) 6⅜ in.

Probably from the sounding board of the 1787 pulpit in the first meeting house in Berlin, Mass. Some of the leaves are restored.

Private collection

83

INTERIOR VIEW

"Town Meeting"

Elkanah Tisdale, b. ca. 1771

New York and Connecticut, ca. 1795

Line engraving; H. 5¾ in., w. 3½ in.

Published in John Trumbull, *McFingal* (New York, 1795), op-

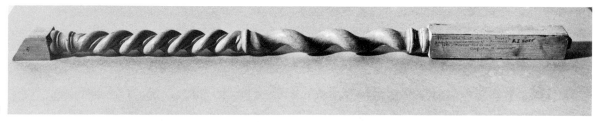

posite p. 16. Shows the moderator conducting the meeting from the pulpit. His hand rests on a pulpit cushion.
Massachusetts Historical Society, Boston, Mass.

Pew fragments, accessories, and plans

84
BOX PEW
Ludlow, Mass., ca. 1797 or early nineteenth century
Pine, maple; unpainted;
H. 43½ in., L. 74½ in., w. 71½ in.
From the Ludlow meeting house, erected in 1783.
The pew may have been assembled from the remnants of several box pews from the same building.
First Parish Church, Ludlow, Mass.

85
PEW DOOR AND PEW END
Attributed to John Norman, 1612–1672, or his son John, Jr., 1637–1713

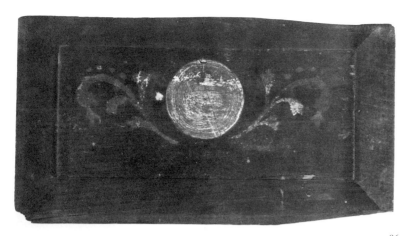

86

Marblehead, Mass., ca. 1659
Oak; door: H. 38¼ in.,
w. 20¼ in.; end: H. 38½ in.,
w. 25¼ in.
"32" painted on white oval in
upper left panel of door.
Drilled holes for spindles in upper
rails. By tradition, thought to
have been made for the first meeting house in Marblehead, built in
1659, then reused in the second
meeting house of 1695, which was
demolished in 1824. These two
fragments together with another
pair constitute the largest group
of joined interior woodwork to
survive from seventeenth-century
New England.
Marblehead Historical Society,
Marblehead, Mass. 648

86
PANEL FROM PEW
Dorchester, Mass., mid-
eighteenth century
Pine; painted blue and yellow;
H. 7¼ in., w. 14 in.

From the fourth meeting house of
the First Church in Dorchester
(1744–1817).
The Society for the Preservation
of New England Antiquities, Boston, Mass. 8.1919

87
PEW DOOR
Bolton, Mass., ca. 1793
Pine, maple; painted off-white;
H. 42⅜ in., w. 20½ in.
"23" painted in black.
From the second meeting house
in Bolton, completed in 1793 and
remodeled in 1844.
Private collection

88
PEW DOOR
Farmington, Conn., ca. 1828
Pine, iron hinges; painted oak
grain; H. 31½ in., w. 15 in.
"XIII" painted in gold.
From the 1828 renovation of the
1771 building.

First Church of Christ
Congregational, 1652,
Farmington, Conn.

89
PEW DOOR
Plymouth, Mass., 1831
Pine, mahogany, brass numeral
1; painted oak grain; H. 40¾ in.,
w. 18½ in.
From a slip pew of the fourth
meeting house of the First Church
in Plymouth (1831–1892).
First Parish Church in Plymouth,
Mass.

90
SPINDLE FROM PEW RAILING
Ipswich, Mass., mid-eighteenth
century
Mahogany; L. 9¼ in.,
DIAM. 1½ in.
Label with the spindle states that
it came from John Harris's pew in
the "Old First Church, Ipswich,
Mass.," probably the fourth meet-
ing house (1749–1846).
The Society for the Preservation
of New England Antiquities, Bos-
ton, Mass. 1973.216

91
PEW SPINDLE
Massachusetts, ca. 1750–1800
Maple; unpainted; L. 9¼ in.
From the First Church of
Hamilton (Ipswich Hamlet),
Mass., built in 1714.
Essex Institute, Salem, Mass.
2,623

90

91

92

93

92
PEW SPINDLE
Massachusetts, ca. 1750–1800
Maple; painted green; L. 7⅛ in.
From East Church, Salem,
Mass., built in 1718
Essex Institute, Salem, Mass.
105.222.8

93
PEW SPINDLE
Massachusetts, ca. 1750–1800
Maple; unpainted; L. 8½ in.
Paper label: "Part of a pew from
the meeting-house of the Second
/ Congregational Church, Mug-
ford St., Marblehead. Built /
1716; taken down 1830 [actually
1832] Indorsed by Hon. J. J. H.
/ Gregory of Marblehead, whose
father purchased the / Meeting
House. / — Price, 15 cents. —"
Essex Institute, Salem, Mass.
106.608.1

94
PEW SHELF BRACKET
Worcester, Mass., ca. 1763
Pine; inside painted bright green;
L. 3⅜ in., W. 1⅜ in.
Fragment from the second meet-
ing house in Worcester, erected in
1763.
Worcester Historical Museum,
Worcester, Mass. 1979.605

95
ARMREST
Probably Maine, eighteenth
century
Maple; H. 7 in., W. 6½ in.,
D. 3½ in.
Thought to have been used in the
First Parish Church, York,
Maine.
Old Gaol Museum, York, Me.
1977.79

96
PEW ARMREST
Connecticut, ca. 1815–1835
Maple, maple and mahogany

veneer; H. 11½ in., L. 12¾ in.,
W. 4⅜ in.
Branded "G STILLMAN" twice on
underside.
Part of mahogany banding and
veneered edge missing. Probably
belonged to George Stillman
(1774–1846) of Wethersfield,
Conn., or his son of the same
name (1798–1882), who also was
a deacon of the Congregational
Church in Wethersfield in 1856.
Wethersfield Historical Society,
Wethersfield, Conn.

97

WRITING ARM
Massachusetts, late eighteenth
century
Pine, maple, oak; unpainted;
L. 18¼ in., W. 6⅝ in. (L. of
support, 18¼ in.)
Formerly attached to a pew side,
probably in the fourth meeting
house of the First Church in Ipswich (1749–1846).
First Church in Ipswich, Mass.

98

98

PEW CUSHION
William Hancock, active ca.
1796–ca. 1849
Boston, Mass., ca. 1825–1829
Red wool damask, hair stuffing;
L. 50 in., W. 11 in., D. 3 in.
Paper label: "MADE BY / WILLIAM
HANCOCK / UPHOSTERER, / 39, 41
& 45 MARKET-STREET, / BOS-
TON, / Where may be had all
Kinds of Upholstery Goods — /
and the business as usually at-
tended to in all its branches."
Probably the seat cushion from a
set of four which included another
seat cushion and two back cush-
ions.
The Society for the Preservation
of New England Antiquities, Boston, Mass. 1976.174.1

99

FABRIC REMNANT
Probably England, ca. 1800–
1825
Olive-green silk brocade with
cream, pink, and green flowers;
L. 25 in., W. 18½ in.
From a mahogany armrest in a
church in Newburyport, Mass.,
probably the First Presbyterian
Church, founded in 1755.
Essex Institute, Salem, Mass.
108,607

100

FABRIC REMNANT
Probably England, ca. 1832
Red wool damask;
L. 11¾ in., W. 3 in.
From an original pew covering in
the Crombie Street Church,
Salem, Mass., built in 1832.
Essex Institute, Salem, Mass.
126,524

101

FOOTSTOOL
Massachusetts, early nineteenth
century
Pine; painted brown with yellow
stripes; H. 7 in., L. 10⅞ in.,
W. 6⅞ in.
Used in a pew of the second meet-
ing house in Leominster, Mass.
(1775–1823).
Leominster Historical Society,
Leominster, Mass.

102

SPIT BOX
Massachusetts, early nineteenth
century
Pine; H. 3 in., L. 8¾ in.,
W. 8½ in.
Thought to be one of two purchased in 1826 from Amory Sawyer of Berlin, Mass., for 17 cents
each. Bought for the second meet-

101

103

ing house in Berlin, as part of the building's original furnishings. Private collection

103
FOOT WARMER
New England, eighteenth century
Oak, iron; H. 6 in., L. 7¾ in., w. 7¼ in.
"This Foot Stove was presented by Edwin Hall of West Hartford Conn. May 20. 1865. Was in use in 1740" on label pasted to top. Ceramic pot to hold coals is no longer with the stove.
Connecticut Historical Society, Hartford, Conn. A–154

104
FOOT WARMER
New England, early nineteenth century
Walnut, tin; H. 5⅞ in., L. 9⅛ in., w. 7⅝ in.
Brass plate inscribed "To / the Essex Institute / Foot Stove, container for live coals, perforated heart design on four sides; / used at Church by our Grandmother Mrs. Ebenezer T. [Ruth Hewes] Abbott / North Reading, Massachusetts. (1830's–1840's) / Gift of Sidney Howard Carney, Jr., 1942"
Essex Institute, Salem, Mass. 125,216

105
FOOT WARMER
New England, early nineteenth century

142

Pine, walnut, tin;
H. 5½ in., DIAM. 9 in.
"S. Derby / Pew no. 7 / 1820"
in ink on bottom.
Includes inside a tin container
for hot coals.
Essex Institute, Salem, Mass.
111,055

106
PEW PLAN
Wenham, Mass., early
nineteenth century
Ink on paper;
H. 7¾ in., W. 12⅝ in.
Pew plan of the third meeting
house in Wenham, Mass. (1748–
1843).
Wenham Historical Association
and Museum, Wenham, Mass.

107
PEW PLAN
Wethersfield, Conn., 1824
Ink on paper; H. 7¾ in., W. 8½
Dated January 12, 1824 on
reverse side.
Plan of First Church of Christ,
Wethersfield, Conn.
Wethersfield Historical Society,
Wethersfield, Conn.

108
TWO PEW RECEIPTS
Manuscript; dated Newbury,
Mass., February 21, 1824
Sale of 1/3 interest in pew 27 of
the First Church in Ipswich by
Daniel Noyes to John H.
Boardman.
Printed form; dated Salem,
Mass., December 14, 1825

104

105

143

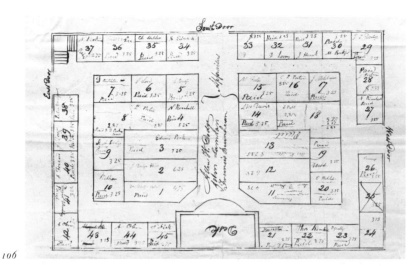

106

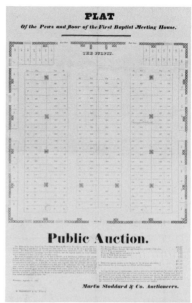

109

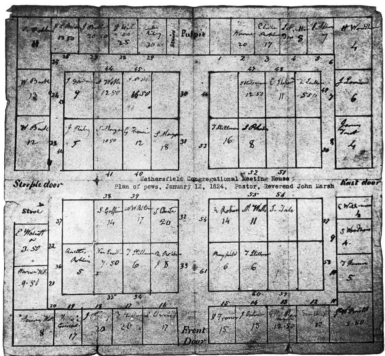

107

109
BROADSIDE POSTER
Providence, R.I., 1832
Ink on paper; H. 24 in.,
W. 20 in. (frame)
Printed advertisement for the
public auction of pews at the First
Baptist Church, Providence.
Printer: W. Marshall and Com-
pany, 1832
First Baptist Church in America,
Providence, R.I.

Sale of 1/3 interest in pew 27 of
the First Church in Ipswich by
David Pulsifer and his wife Eliz-

abeth to John How Boardman.
First Church in Ipswich, Mass.

Meetinghouse-related objects and documents

110
HOURGLASS
New England, eighteenth century
Mahogany, glass; H. 7⅞ in.,
DIAM. 3⅝ in.
First Congregational Church of Woodstock, Conn.

111
PHOTOGRAPH OF HOURGLASS FRAME
From glass-plate negative
First Congregational Church of Woodstock, Conn.

112
HOURGLASS
Probably England, eighteenth century
Oak, walnut, glass;
H. 7½ in., DIAM. 3½ in.
Belonged to Ebenezer Morse, minister of the Congregational Church in Boylston, Mass., from 1743 to 1773, when he was dismissed because of his Tory leanings.
Old Sturbridge Village, Sturbridge, Mass.

113
FIRE BUCKET
New England, ca. 1829
Leather, iron rings; painted green; H. 18 in., DIAM. 9 in.
"First Parish / N°. 2 / 1829"

110

112

painted in yellow and black.
First Parish Church in Exeter, N.H.

114
NOTICE BOX
Massachusetts, probably late eighteenth century
Pine; painted gray-blue;
H. 12¼ in., W. 10 in., D. 2¾ in.
Contains the following announcement: "The Intention of Marriage

between/ Mr. Benjamin Hilton and Miss Elizabeth/Mors both of Beverly are hereby/ Published by me/ Beverly May 11th 1794/ Joseph Wood F. Chur."
The Beverly Historical Society, Beverly, Mass.

115
POOR BOX
Massachusetts, late eighteenth or
early nineteenth century
Oak, brass fittings; H. 10⅜ in.,
L. 4⅛ in., W. 4 in.
Thought to have been made or
provided by William Harris, rec-
tor of St. Michael's Church, Mar-
blehead, Mass., from 1791 to
1802.
St. Michael's Church Archives,
Marblehead, Mass.

116
DRUM
New England, late seventeenth
century
Oak, walnut; H. 19⅝ in.,
DIAM. 23¾ in.
"L D" in brass tacks on outside.
"Drum anciently used to call peo-
ple together on the Sabbath and
on other public occasions. Pre-
sented by the family of the late
Mr. William Porter to the Histor-
ical Society of Connecticut 1842"
inscribed on label applied to
drum. Used in Farmington,
Conn., as a warning drum.
Connecticut Historical Society,
Hartford, Conn. A-1719

117
CONCH SHELL
Probably from the West Indies
L. 8¼ in., DIAM. 9⅜ in.
Used by the town of Whately,
Mass., to summon people to
meetings, from about 1773 to
1795.
First Congregational Church of
Whately, Mass.

113

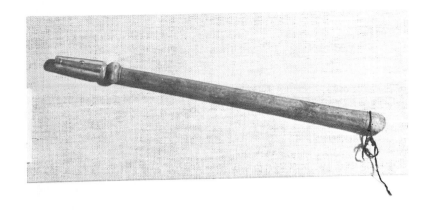

115

118

118
TITHING STICK
Probably Massachusetts,
eighteenth century
Maple, brass-tipped;
L. 24 in., W. 1⅜ in.
Found in Bolton, Mass.
Private collection

119
TITHING STICK
Connecticut, eighteenth or early
nineteenth century
Hickory; L. 60⅛ in.,
DIAM. (swelled end) 1¼ in.
Holes drilled in end may have
held feathers. Tithing stick de-
scended in the family of a deacon
of the Rocky Hill Congregational
Church with the understanding
that it was used in that church.
Rocky Hill Historical Society,
Rocky Hill, Conn.

120
TITHING STICK
New Hampshire, eighteenth or
early nineteenth century
Probably maple; painted reddish-
brown; L. 55 in., DIAM. 2½ in.
From Walpole, N.H., but with-
out specific meetinghouse associ-
ations.
Private collection

121
WALL SCONCE
New England, ca. 1775–1825
Tin with glass chimney; painted
dark green or black. Sconce:
H. 13½ in., W. 4½ in.,
D. 3½ in.; chimney: H. 8⅜ in.,
DIAM. 2 in.
Found in a wall cavity created
during the 1833 rebuilding of St.
Michael's Church, Marblehead,
Mass.
St. Michael's Church Archives,
Marblehead, Mass.

122
CANDELABRA
America, ca. 1794 or early
nineteenth century
Tin; H. 32 in., SPAN 44 in.
From St. Matthew's Episcopal
Church, East Plymouth, Conn.,
consecrated in 1795. Restored in
1961.
Connecticut Historical Society,
Hartford, Conn. A-2101

123
CHANDELIER
New England, early nineteenth
century
Tin; H. 15 in., DIAM. 29 in.
Formerly used in the 1819 meet-
ing house or vestry of the First
Church in Hancock, N.H.
Hancock Historical Society, Han-
cock, N.H.

124

FRAGMENT FROM INTERIOR
PAINTING
Attributed to John Gibbs, active
1729–1756
Boston, Mass., ca. 1755
Oil on canvas; H. 14½ in.,
W. 27¾ in. (sight)
Believed to have been removed
from the first Trinity Church
building (1735) when the second
building was erected in 1829.
This is one of three fragments
from this painting which have re-
cently come to light.
Trinity Church in the City of
Boston, Mass. Given in memory
of Robert Hallowell Gardiner

125

STATUE
"The Angel Gabriel"
Massachusetts, ca. 1797
Pine; painted ivory over grayish-
white; H. 33 in., W. 19 in.,
D. 11 in.
Installed in a niche behind the
pulpit in the second meeting
house in Royalston, Mass.
(1797–1851).
The First Congregational Church
of Royalston, Mass.

126

SIGNED PETITION
Kennebunk, Maine, 1771
Ink on paper: H. 7½ in.,
W. 6¾ in.
Letter, signed April 6, 1771, call-
ing a meeting to discuss building
a new, more convenient meeting
house.
First Parish, Unitarian, Kenne-
bunk, Me.

121

122

123

James was Benjamin Franklin's older brother.
Worcester Art Museum, Goodspeed Collection, Worcester, Mass. G 3468

Meetinghouse furniture

128
BAPTISMAL STAND
Massachusetts, late seventeenth century
Maple; painted black over green; H. 40 in., DIAM. (top) 13½ in.
Said to have been used in the First Church in Salem. Owned at one time by Benjamin Gerrish, a deacon of that church.
Essex Institute, Salem, Mass. 1,781

129
COMMUNION TABLE
Attributed to Stephen Jacques, 1661–1744
Newbury, Mass., ca. 1700
Oak; H. 30 in., L. 42⅜ in., W. 37⅞ in.
Believed to have been made for the First Parish of Newbury at the time that the fourth meeting house was erected by Stephen Jacques.
Historical Society of Old Newbury, Newbury, Mass.

127
BROADSIDE
"Divine Examples of God's Severe Judgments upon Sabbath Breakers"

James Franklin, 1696?–1735
Boston, Mass., 1718
Printed woodcut; H. 17⅝ in., W. 13⅝ in.
"J. F. Sculp." in lower right.

130
COMMUNION TABLE
Probably Massachusetts, ca. 1725–1750
Pine; stripped of paint;

149

130

H. 33⅛ in., L. 53½ in.,
w. 29⅜ in.
Used in the first (1723–1766) and
second (built 1766) meeting
houses in Shrewsbury, Mass.
Traces of a light blue-gray paint
indicate its probable original
color, which may also have
matched the pulpit color of the
second meeting house.
Private collection

131
COMMUNION TABLE
Jacob Fisher, Jr.
Lancaster, Mass., 1826
Mahogany; H. 33½ in.,
w. 51 in., D. 26⅝ in.
Table was purchased along with
two armchairs for the new meeting house of the First Church in
Berlin, Mass., in 1826. A bill presented by Jacob Fisher for this table is in the archives of the town
of Berlin.
Private collection
150

132
SIDE CHAIR
Probably Massachusetts, ca.
1720–1740
Maple, ash, reupholstered in
linen; H. 45¼ in., w. 18⅛ in.,
D. 17¾ in.
"A chair first used in Westboro
Meeting House. Their small
house 100 year since. Bot of the
Misses Johnson in 1860 May 12"
was inscribed on the bottom. The
chair probably had a rush or
splint seat originally.
Worcester Historical Museum,
Worcester, Mass. 1933.52

133
SIDE CHAIR
Probably New Hampshire, late
eighteenth century
Maple, ash, rush seat; painted
black; H. 45¼ in., w. 19 in.,
D. 14½ in.
Brass plaque: "Pulpit Chair from

/ Original Meeting-house / Gift
of Mary F. Emery"
Probably used in the fourth meet-
ing house of the Congregational
Church in Exeter, N.H. (1730–
1798). Bottom of feet restored.
First Parish Church in Exeter,
N.H.

134
DEACONS' BENCH
Massachusetts, ca. 1790–1810
Pine, maple, iron stays; painted
black over green; H. 35½ in.,
w. 36¼ in., D. 18½ in.
One of a pair. The bench resembles another bench, over eight feet
long, that was used in 1812 during
the ordination and commissioning
of the first group of missionaries
sent to Asia by the Tabernacle
Church.
Tabernacle Church, Salem,
Mass.

135
ARMCHAIR
Joseph Wilder, 1787–1825
New Ipswich, N.H., ca. 1821
Pine, maple arms; H. 36½ in.,
w. 18½ in., D. 16¾ in.
"J. WILDER" stamped on
underside of seat
One of a pair of chairs said to have
been given for use in a New
Hampshire church that was ded-
icated in 1821.
Private collection

136
DEACON'S CHAIR

Massachusetts, ca. 1832
Unidentified wood, rose-colored brocade upholstery; painted black; H. 54¼ in., W. 24⅜ in., D. 20¾ in.
Brass plaque: "Chair from First Church 1830 / Given in Memory of / CHARLES and RUSSELL DAVIS."
One of a pair. They were made for the fifth building of the First Church in Plymouth, which was completed on December 14, 1831.
First Parish Church in Plymouth, Mass.

137
READING DESK

Southern New England, early nineteenth century
Pine, maple, walnut lid, tulip; grain painted to imitate striped maple; H. 48¼ in., W. 37 in., D. 24 in.
Thought to have been used in Southington, Conn. The location of reading desks in meeting houses is unknown, but they probably provided an alternative to the pulpit for conducting parts of meetings or services. The level of the writing surface has been raised by an addition to the case.
Barnes Museum, Southington, Conn.

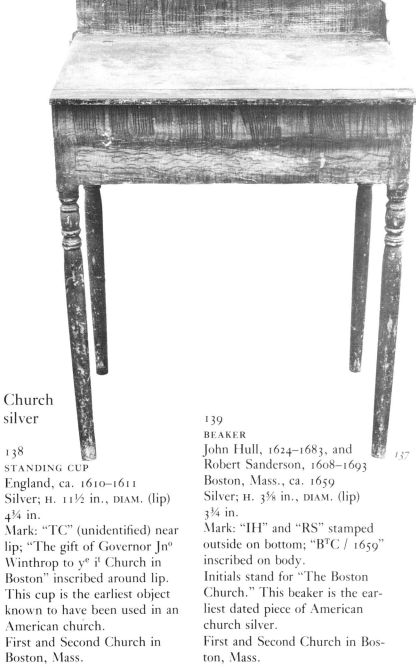

137

Church silver

138
STANDING CUP

England, ca. 1610–1611
Silver; H. 11½ in., DIAM. (lip) 4¾ in.
Mark: "TC" (unidentified) near lip; "The gift of Governor Jnᵒ Winthrop to yᵉ iᵗ Church in Boston" inscribed around lip. This cup is the earliest object known to have been used in an American church.
First and Second Church in Boston, Mass.

139
BEAKER

John Hull, 1624–1683, and Robert Sanderson, 1608–1693
Boston, Mass., ca. 1659
Silver; H. 3⅝ in., DIAM. (lip) 3¾ in.
Mark: "IH" and "RS" stamped outside on bottom; "BᵀC / 1659" inscribed on body.
Initials stand for "The Boston Church." This beaker is the earliest dated piece of American church silver.
First and Second Church in Boston, Mass.

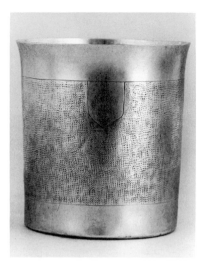

139

140

TWO-HANDLED CUP

John Hull, 1624–1683, and
Robert Sanderson, 1608–1693
Boston, Mass., ca. 1660–1678
Silver; H. 3⅛ in., DIAM. 3½ in.
Marks: "IH" and "RS" near lip;
inscriptions: "A^C E" on body;
"The Gift of Mrs. Elizabeth
Clement to the Church in Dor-
chester 1678" on back of neck;
"Presented by the First Church
Dorchester, to the Second
Church. Jan 1st 1878" on front of
neck.
Second Church in Dorchester,
Mass.

141

STANDING CUP WITH LID

Francis Garthorne, 1675?–1726
London, England, ca. 1694
Silver; cup: H. 8¼ in.,
DIAM. (lip) 4⅝ in.; lid: H. 1⅜ in.,
DIAM. 5¼ in.
Mark: "FG" near lip; "The Gift
of K William & Q Mary to y^e
Reve^d Sam^ll Myles for ye use of
their Maj^ties Chappell in
N:England : 1694" inscribed on
bottom; arms of William Rex on
body.
A silver flagon accompanied this
gift. More royal gifts of commun-
ion silver were made to King's
Chapel, Boston, in 1697 and again
in 1772, when this standing cup
and the flagon were given to
Christ Church, Cambridge.
Christ Church, Cambridge,
Mass.

142

BAPTISMAL BASIN

Jeremiah Dummer, 1645–1718
Boston, Mass., ca. 1695
Silver; DIAM. 14⅞ in., DEPTH
2⅝ in.
Mark: "ID" on rim; "Ex Dono
Pupillarum, 1695" and "A Baptis-
mall Bassin consecrated, be-
queath^d & presented to the
Church of Christ in Cambridge,
his Dearly beloved Flock, by the
Rev^d. Mr Wm Brattle Past^r of the
S^d church: Who was translated
from his Charge to his Crown,
Febr 15:1716/17" inscribed on
rim.
The First Parish in Cambridge,
Mass.

141

143

TANKARD
Edward Winslow, 1669–1753
Boston, Mass., ca. 1703
Silver; H. 6¾ in., DIAM. (base)
4⅞ in.
Mark: "EW" near lip to left of
handle; "The gift of / Capt. Richard Sprague / to the Church of
Charlstoune 1703" inscribed out-
side on bottom; "This / TANKARD
/ with three large Flaggons where
given / to the Church in Charles-
town / by / Richard SPRAGUE,
Esqr / a liberal Benefactor to the
Church & poor of / said Town
A.D. 1703. The Flaggons not
being needed / for Sacramental
uses, were sold by Vote of the
Church / June 17th 1800 & the
property vested in a Town note
/ see Chh. Book No Folio 1, p. 58,
& Chh. Book No 2, 4+0. p. 31.";
Chester arms engraved on body.
Chester was the surname of
Sprague's first wife. Sprague bequeathed £100 to be "invested
into four Sylver tankards for ye
Sacramentall use and ye rest of sd
sum to be disposed of by ye Deacons." The church sold this tankard in 1926.
The Henry Francis du Pont Winterthur Museum, Winterthur,
Del. 59.3365

144

BEAKER
John Edwards, 1671–1746
Boston, Mass., ca. 1716
Silver; H. 4⅛ in., DIAM. (lip)
3⅜ in.

Mark: "IE"; "The gift of the
Barnstable Church 1716." in-
scribed on body.
First Congregational Church of
Canterbury, Conn.

145

BEAKER OR CUP
John Coney, 1656–1722
Boston, Mass., ca. 1713
Silver; H. 4¼ in., DIAM. (lip)
3¾ in.
Mark: "IC" near lip and outside
on bottom; "Hamptn Old Chh
1713" inscribed outside on bottom.
One of eight. Three pewter flagons and one pewter tankard were
also part of this communion service.
Private collection

146

BEAKER OR CUP
Jacob Hurd, 1703–1758
Boston, Mass., ca. 1744
Silver; H. 4¼ in., DIAM. (lip)
3⅞ in.
Mark: "I HURD" near lip;
"Hampton Old Church / 1744"
inscribed outside on bottom.
One of four. Purchased at the
same time as four pewter flagons
(Catalogue no. 162).
Private collection

147

PLATE
Edward Winslow, 1669–1753
Boston, Mass., ca. 1711
Silver; DIAM. 15⅛ in., DEPTH
1¾ in.

147

Mark: "EW" on rim; Foster arms
on rim.
Bequeathed to the North (Second)
Church in Boston by Abigail Foster. The plate matches two others
given in the same year by Thomas
and Edward Hutchinson.
First and Second Church in Boston, Mass.

148

BEAKER WITH HANDLE ADDED
John Coney, 1656–1722
Boston, Mass., ca. 1718
Silver; H. 5⅞ in., DIAM. (lip)
4¼ in.
Mark: "IC"; "The gift of Robt
Brisco 1718" inscribed on body.
The handle, which came from a
two-handled cup owned by the
same church (Catalogue no. 149),
was applied to this beaker by
Israel Trask, who billed the
church $1.75 on November 29,
1809.
First Parish Unitarian Church,
Beverly, Mass.

149
TWO-HANDLED CUP OR BEAKER WITH HANDLE REMOVED
Attributed to John Blowers, 1710–1748
Boston, Mass., ca. 1729
Silver; H. 5⅜ in., DIAM. (base) 3⅝ in.
"The Legacy of the Rev^nd Mr Tho: Blowers / To the First Church in Beverly / Dec^d: June the 17th 1729" inscribed on body. See Catalogue no. 148. The attribution of this unmarked piece of silver is based on the fact that John Blowers was the donor's son. First Parish Unitarian Church, Beverly, Mass.

150
FLAGON
John Potwine, 1698–1792
Boston, Mass., ca. 1720–1730
Silver; H. 13⅝ in., DIAM. (base) 6⅝ in.
Mark: "I•Potwine" near lip to left of handle; "The Gift of Mrs Mary Lemon / TO THE / 1st Church of Christ / IN / Charlstowne" inscribed on body.
Winged cherub heads similar to the two engraved on this flagon appear in other meetinghouse-related objects, but they also decorate examples of needlework and domestic interiors. Yale University Art Gallery, Mabel Brady Garvan Collection, New Haven, Conn.

150a

TANKARD
John Burt, 1693–1745
Boston, Mass., ca. 1740–1745
Silver; H. 7½ in., DIAM. (base)
4⅞ in.
Mark: "JOHN BURT"; "The
half of this Vessel was given to /
the first Church of Christ in Bev-
erly / by Capᵗ I • Herrick and his
two Sons / and the other half by
Deacon I • Wood / and his two
Sons / H • H . I • H . 1747 I • W
. I • W" inscribed on body.
The gift was acknowledged by the
church on December 16, 1747,
two years after the maker of the
tankard died.
First Parish Unitarian Church,
Beverly, Mass.

152

BEAKER
Nathaniel Hurd, 1729–1777
Boston, Mass., ca. 1764
Silver, H. 6⅝ in., DIAM. (lip)
4⅝ in.
Mark: "N•Hurd"; "The Gift of
the Honorable / Thomas HAN-
COCK Esq. to the/Church of
Christ in Lexington / 1764" in-
scribed on body with Hancock
coat of arms.
First Parish in Lexington, Mass.

153
MUG
John Coburn, 1725–1803
Boston, Mass., ca. 1775

Silver; H. 5 in., DIAM. (lip) 3⅜ in.
Mark: "J Coburn" outside on
bottom; "EX DONO / JUVENUM
ALIQUORUM / REVDO SAMUELI

152

155

DEANE / PASTORI FIDELISSIMO / 1775." inscribed on body. Presented to the Rev. Samuel Deane, pastor of the First Parish in Falmouth (now Portland), Maine, from 1764 to 1814, by twenty-one young men of the parish whose initials are engraved on the bottom. It was purchased in a local jewelry store about 1850 and donated to the church in 1876.
First Parish Church, Portland, Me.

154
PLATE OR PATEN
Jeremiah Dummer, 1645–1718
Boston, Mass., ca. 1670–1718
Silver; DIAM. 9⅛ in., DEPTH ⅞ in.
Mark: "ID" on rim; "N^CE" inscribed on back; "This plate was given me at my birth / by my Grand Father / Nath^ll Cary Esqr" inscribed around arms of Mills of Harscombe in Gloucestershire and "KING'S CHAPEL / 1798" on rim.

This plate remained in private ownership for almost 100 years before it was donated to the church.
King's Chapel, Boston, Mass.

155
BEAKER
Samuel Shethar, active ca. 1782–1808
Litchfield, Conn., ca. 1800
Silver; H. 4½ in., DIAM. (lip) 3⅜ in.
"A present from M^r./ JOSIAH BRONSON / to the Church of / CRIST, in / Middlebury / AE 88" inscribed on one side; "Given / Sept / AD 1800 / price / £4=6=0" on the other; "S••Shethar" scratched on bottom.
First Congregational Church in Middlebury, Conn.

156
BREAD BASKET
Probably Newburyport, Mass., ca. 1805
Silver; L. 14¾ in., W. 10 in., D. 1¾ in.
Mark: "MOULTON" on underside (unidentified); "Property of / the NORTH CHURCH, in / SALE. / 1805" inscribed on bottom.
North Church split from the First Church in Salem in 1773 and rejoined it in 1923.
First Church in Salem, Mass.

157

157
GOBLET OR CHALICE
New England, ca. 1839
Plated silver; H. 6⅜ in., DIAM. (lip) 4½ in.
One of six. Part of a communion service that includes two flagons, one large plate, and two smaller plates (Catalogue no. 158). Used by the First Universalist Society in Lynn, Mass., from 1839 to 1873.
First Universalist Society in Greater Lynn, Swampscott, Mass.

154

158

158
PLATE
New England, ca. 1839
Plated silver; DIAM. 10¼ in.
Part of the same communion service as Catalogue no. 157.
First Universalist Society in Greater Lynn, Swampscott, Mass.

Church pewter

159
BEAKER
England, seventeenth century
Pewter; H. 5⅜ in., DIAM. (lip) 3¾ in.
Several sets of initials scratched on bottom of base.
Said to be a "communion cup or beaker brought over from England in 1660 by Deacon Enoch Eaton" of Salisbury, N.H.
New Hampshire Historical Society, Concord, N.H. 1839.2

160
FLAGON
England, early eighteenth century
Pewter; H. 15 in., DIAM. (base) 7⅝ in.
Marks: "IN" inside on bottom, four touchmarks near lip to right of handle; "The Gift of John Hall Esq / to the Second Church in / Wallingford / 1725" inscribed on front.
Earliest dated piece of church pewter used in America.
Connecticut Historical Society, Hartford, Conn. A-2110

161
PAIR OF BEAKERS
Attributed to Robert Bonynge, 1731–63
Boston, Mass., ca. 1743
Pewter; H. 5¼ in., DIAM. (lip) 3⅝ in.
"The Gift of mr Samuel Parkman / To the Church in Nottingham 1743" inscribed on one beaker, "The Gift of mr Daniel Emery / To the Church in Nottingham 1743" on the other.
New Hampshire Historical Society, Concord, N.H. 1915.5.3-.4

162
FLAGON
England, ca. 1744
Pewter; H. 13⅛ in., DIAM. (base) 6½ in.
One of four flagons purchased by the church in Hampton, N.H., in 1744, along with four silver beak-

ers (Catalogue no. 146).
Private collection

163
BEAKER OR TUMBLER
William Calder, 1792–1856
Providence, R.I., ca. 1825–1850
Pewter; H. 3⅛ in., DIAM. (lip) 3⅛ in.
Mark: "CALDER" inside on bottom.
The same mold used to make the body of this beaker was used for the goblet (Catalogue no. 164) and the nursing bottle (Catalogue no. 165).
Dr. and Mrs. Melvyn D. Wolf

164
GOBLET OR CHALICE
Attributed to William Calder, 1792–1856
Providence, R.I., ca. 1825–1850
Pewter; H. 6 in., DIAM. (base) 3¾ in.
The cup part of this goblet is from the same mold used for the beaker (Catalogue no. 163) and the nursing bottle (Catalogue no. 165).
Private collection

165
NURSING BOTTLE
Attributed to William Calder, 1792–1856
Providence, R.I., ca. 1825–1850
Pewter; H. 5½ in., DIAM. 3¼ in.
The body of the nursing bottle was made from the same mold as were the beaker (Catalogue no. 163) and the cup part of the goblet (Catalogue no. 164).
Private collection

166
FLAGON
William Calder, 1792–1856
Providence, R.I., ca. 1825–1850
Pewter; H. 11⅜ in., DIAM. (base)
5⅞ in.
Mark: "CALDER" outside on
bottom.
Believed to have been used in a
church in Rhode Island. The
body of the flagon is from the
same mold as the teapot (Cata-
logue no. 167).
Private collection

167
TEAPOT
William Calder, 1792–1856
Providence, R.I., ca. 1825–1850
Pewter; H. 10⅞ in., DIAM. (base)
5⅞ in.
Mark: "CALDER" outside on
bottom.
The body of this teapot comes
from the same mold as the flagon
(Catalogue no. 166).
Private collection

168
GOBLET OR CHALICE
Israel Trask, 1786–1867
Beverly, Mass., ca. 1825–1849
Pewter; H. 7 in., DIAM. (lip)
3⅞ in.
Mark: "I•TRASK" inside base.
One of six; the five others are all
unmarked. Part of a communion
service used in the early nine-
teenth century by the Kennebunk
First Parish until it was replaced
by a silver-plated service acquired
in 1850.
First Parish, Unitarian, Kenne-
bunk, Me.

160

169

FLAGON

Israel Trask, 1786–1867
Beverly, Mass., ca. 1825–1849
Pewter; H. 12½ in., DIAM. (base)
6 in.
Mark: "I•TRASK" outside on
bottom.
One of a pair. Part of the same
communion service as Catalogue
no. 168. The lid of this flagon was
made from the same mold as the

base of the goblet.
First Parish, Unitarian, Kennebunk, Me.

170

FIFTEEN-PIECE COMMUNION
SERVICE

PAIR OF FLAGONS

England, ca. 1760–1790
Pewter; H. 10⅛ in., DIAM. (base)
5½ in.

PAIR OF TANKARDS

Robert Bush, active ca. 1765–
1790
Bristol, England, ca. 1765–1790
Pewter; H. 7½ in., DIAM. (base)
5⅛ in.
Mark: "Robert Bush" inside on
bottom.

PAIR OF GOBLETS

England or New England, late
eighteenth century

168

169

Pewter; H. 8½ in., DIAM. (lip)
3⅝ in.

SIX BEAKERS
Attributed to Robert Bonynge,
active 1731–ca. 1763 and later
Boston, Mass., ca. 1765
Pewter; H. 5¼ in., DIAM. (lip)
3¾ in.
Mark: "RB" inside on bottom.

160

TWO LARGE PLATES
England or New England, ca.
1765–1790
Pewter; DIAM. 15⅛ in.

BASIN
Nathaniel Austin, 1741–1816
Charlestown, Mass., 1763–1807
Pewter; DIAM. 8⅛ in., D. 2⅛ in.
Mark: Eagle touch inside on bot-
tom.

The Westmoreland Congregational Society of the Park Hill
Church, Westmoreland, N.H.

171
TWO COMMUNION TOKENS
New England, ca. 1807 and
1824
Pewter; left: L. ⅞ in., W. ⅞ in.;
right: L. 1 in., W. ⅞ in.
Inscriptions: "A ÷ C / H ÷ N" on
obverse, "1807" on reverse of left
token; "A. C. / of / Hebron" on
obverse, "J. I. / July 7. / 1824" on
reverse of right token.
"A. C." probably stands for "Anglican Church"; "Hebron" is
probably Hebron, Conn., where
the Church of England was established in 1735.
Private collection

172
TRAVELING COMMUNION SET
New England, early nineteenth
century
Pewter, leather case with red
velvet lining, brass and iron
fittings; beaker: H. 2⅞ in.,
DIAM. 3 in.; paten: DIAM. 3¾ in.,
DEPTH 1⅛ in.
Probably used by a Presbyterian
minister who served a number of
small rural towns.
The Reverend and Mrs. Clare
Milton Ingham

170

171a

171b

162

Other ecclesiastical objects

173
PLATE
Lambeth, England, ca. 1690–1711
Earthenware; blue and white decoration;
DIAM. 8⅞ in., DEPTH 1⅜ in.
Broken and repaired. This plate is the earliest known ceramic object with a history of use in an American house of worship. It was used in the First Church in Concord, Mass., probably to serve the sacramental bread.
Museum of the Concord Antiquarian Society, Concord, Mass.
C-119

174
PAIR OF WINE GLASSES
England, mid-eighteenth century
Lead glass; H. 7½ in., DIAM. (lip) 3½ in.
Label pasted to one glass: "Brought from England about / the year A.D. 1690 by Rev. / Ephraim Woodbridge, and used / in the administration of the / Lords Supper by the first / Congregational Church / established in Groton."
Woodbridge was minister in Groton, Conn., from 1704 to 1724, but the style of the glasses suggests a slightly later date for their acquisition and use.
Connecticut Historical Society, Hartford, Conn. 1.1955.1

175
JUG
Attributed to Daniel Bayley, 1729–1792
Newburyport, Mass., ca. 1763
Red earthenware with black glaze; H. 10¾ in., DIAM. 8⅛ in.
"The Use of Mr. Nobles CHURCH July 10, 1763" inscribed on body. On April 13, 1774, Bayley also published a sermon that Mr. Noble preached on February 8, 1774, "on the nature, use, and end of music in the worship of God." The jug is the earliest dated piece of New England pottery.
Old Gaol Museum, York, Me. 1971.11

176
TWO TANKARDS
New England, eighteenth century
Pine, ash, oak. Left: H. 7¾ in., DIAM. 6 in.; right: H. 9 in., DIAM. 6¼ in.
One of these two tankards was used for communion in the First Parish Church of York, Maine.
Old Gaol Museum, York, Me. 1977.80 and 1977.76

177
PHOTOGRAPH OF COMMUNION CLOTH
Holland, seventeenth century
Linen damask; measurements not available
Depicts Caleb and Joshua returning from the Promised Land. The cloth was used by the Shrewsbury, Mass., church in the eighteenth century.
Henry J. Harlow, Shrewsbury, Mass.

178
COMMUNION CLOTH AND NAPKIN
England or America, early nineteenth century
White linen damask; cloth: L. 51 in., W. 43 in.; napkin: L. 25½ in., W. 25¼ in.
"The blood of Jesus is drink indeed" inscribed in ink on cloth; "Jesus is the bread of life" in ink on napkin.
Probably given to the Rockingham, Vt., Church in 1819 by the Female Society, at the time when a new communion service was purchased by subscription. The gift originally included two napkins.
Rockingham Free Public Library, Bellows Falls, Vt.

179
BAPTISMAL BASIN FRAME
New England, ca. 1740–1825
Iron; painted black and gold; H. 23¼ in., DIAM. 12 in.
Removed from the second meeting house (1740–1826) and preserved in private hands until its reinstallation in the present building (completed 1826) about 1862.
First Parish Church, Portland, Me.

180

181

Ministers' portraits and bands

PORTRAIT
"Mr. Richard Mather"
John Foster, 1648–1681
Cambridge, Mass., ca. 1670
Woodcut; H. 6⅛ in., w. 5⅛ in.
(framed)
A Puritan clergyman who emigrated to New England in 1635, Richard Mather served the Dorchester Church as pastor from 1636 until his death in 1669. He was the progenitor of the Mather family in New England.
Massachusetts Historical Society, Boston, Mass.

180
COLLECTION BOX
Massachusetts, ca. 1775–1825
Pine; painted red; H. 2⅞ in.,
L. 14½ in., w. 5⅛ in.
"L.A." incised outside on bottom.
Used by the Wenham, Mass., Congregational Church.
Wenham Historical Association and Museum, Wenham, Mass.
78.17.1

181
COLLECTION BOX
Probably Rhode Island, early nineteenth century
Cherry; cloth lining; H. 3 in.,
w. 6⅝ in., L. 42 in.
One of several, all with slight variations.
First Baptist Church in America, Providence, R.I.

183
PORTRAIT
"The Reverend Benjamin Colman D.D."
Peter Pelham, 1695–1751
Boston, Mass., 1735
Mezzotint; H. 9⅞ in., w. 7¼ in. (image)
"I. Smibert Pinx" engraved in lower left; "P. Pelham Fecit. / 1735" in lower right.
Engraved portraits of ministers and other local dignitaries were purchased by townspeople for display in their homes. Benjamin Colman (1673–1747) was a minister at the Brattle Square Church, Boston, from its establishment in 1699 until his death in 1747.
Essex Institute, Salem, Mass.
115,627

182

PORTRAIT
"Thomas Prince A.M."
Peter Pelham, 1695–1751
Boston, Mass., 1750
Mezzotint; H. 13⅝ in., w. 9½ in.
(image)
"Jnº Greenwood Pinx." engraved
in lower left; "P. Pelham fecit." in
lower right. Thomas Prince
(1687–1758) was the minister of
the Third Church (Old South) in
Boston from 1718 to 1758.
Essex Institute, Salem, Mass.
106,734

186
PORTRAIT
"Rev. James Cogswell"
Attributed to Joseph Steward,
1753–1822
Hartford, Conn., late 1790s
Oil on canvas; H. 43½ in.,
w. 39¼ in.
James Cogswell (1720–1807) set-
tled in Canterbury, Conn., from
1744 to 1771. He moved to Scot-
land, Conn., in 1772. The white
meeting house in the background
is probably the one erected in
Scotland in 1733.
Private collection

184
PORTRAIT
"The Revᵈ Mʳ William Cooper
of Boston in New England
AE50. 1743" Peter Pelham,
1695–1751
Boston, Mass., 1744
Mezzotint; H. 13⅞ in., w. 9¾ in.
(image)

"I. Smibert Pinx" engraved in
lower left; "P. Pelham fecit" in
lower right. William Cooper
(1694–1743) was a minister at the
Brattle Square Church, Boston,
from 1716 to 1743.
Essex Institute, Salem, Mass.
115,639

The Reverend Benjamin Colman DD

J. Smibert Pinx.

P. Pelham Fecit

183

166

I. Smibert Pinx.   P. Pelham fecit.

The Revᵈ Mʳ William Cooper

of Boston in New-England • Et 50 1743.

Printed for & sold by Step. Whiting at ye Rose & Crown in Union Street Boston

184

167

186

THOMAS PRINCE A.M.

Quintus Ecclesiæ Australis Exjam Novanglorum Pastor e Collegii Harvardini

CANTABRIGIÆ *Curatoribus* SAMUELIS *Armiger Filius et* Thomæ *AM donati Pater*

185

187
MINISTER'S BANDS
England or America, late
eighteenth century
White linen; L. 15⅛ in.,
w. 6⅝ in.
Probably worn by William
Bentley (1759–1819), minister of
the Third Church in Salem,
Mass.
Essex Institute, Salem, Mass.
105,828

188
RUBBING
Slate grave stone of Silas
Bigelow, Paxton, Mass., d. 1769
Worcester, Mass.
Carver: William Young, 1711–
1795
Ink compound on paper;
H. 16½ in., w. 29½ in. (image)
Silas Bigelow was the first minis-
ter of Paxton, Mass., and served
from 1767 to 1769. The stylized,
dentilled pulpit front carved on
his grave stone is similar to the

pulpit surviving from the 1766
meeting house in nearby Shrewsbury, Mass. Rubbing made in
1979 by Ann Parker and Avon
Neal.
Ann Parker and Avon Neal

168

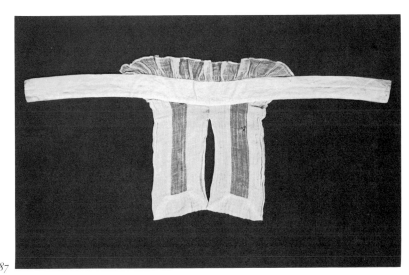

187

188

Music-related objects

189
BASS VIOL
New England, early nineteenth century
Spruce, maple, birch, fruitwood; H. 46 in., W. 18⅛ in., D. 9⅛ in.
"LAUS DEO" painted in yellow on black banner on front; "C. Schmidt 1868 Cleveland" inscribed in pencil inside (probably a repairman).
Formerly owned and played by James Harvey Bingham of Claremont, N.H.
New Hampshire Historical Society, Concord, N.H. 1894.2

190
PITCH PIPE
Scotland or England, ca. 1788
Mahogany, pewter, cork tip; L. 11¼ in., W. 1 in., D. ⅞ in.
"E x O" and "I x S 1788" inscribed on pewter bands.
Inner slide, which adjusts pitch, is marked at intervals with the seven letters of the musical scale. Brought from Scotland to Londonderry, N.H., by the Proctor family.
New Hampshire Historical Society, Concord, N.H. 1966.23.2a & b

191
PITCH PIPE
America or England, ca. 1806
Maple, brass-bound; H. 3 in.,
L. 7 in., W. 1 in.
Used by Eliab Breck, a singing
teacher, in 1806 and mentioned in
the records of the church in Ster-
ling, Mass. Pitch is adjustable.
Sterling Historical Commission,
Sterling, Mass. 00.124
170

192
TWO TUNING FORKS
England or America, nineteenth
century
Iron; left: L. 4⅜ in., W. ⅝ in.;
right: L. 4 in., W. ⅜ in.
Used by the choir director at the
Salisbury Union meeting house in
Salisbury, N.H.
New Hampshire Historical Soci-
ety, Concord, N.H. 1947.32.2a
& b

193
PSALMODY
*The Whole Booke of Psalmes:
Collected into English Meeter*
Thomas Sternhold, d. 1549, and
John Hopkins, active 1550–1560
London, 1614.
Probably used in New England in
the seventeenth century.
Essex Institute, Salem, Mass.

194

PSALMODY

A New Version of the Psalms of David Fitted to the Tunes Used in Churches

Nahum Tate, active 1690–1700, and Nicholas Brady, active 1690–1700

London, 1704. Reprinted Boston, 1720.

The Congregational Library, Boston, Mass.

195

PSALMODY

Psalterium Americanum. The Book of Psalms, In a Translation Exactly conformed unto the Original; but all in Blank Verse.

Cotton Mather, 1663–1728

Boston, 1718.

Inscribed "M. Cutler's." "Thos. Balch's" (crossed out)

At one time owned by Manasseh Cutler, 1742–1823, pastor of the Congregational Church at Hamilton, Mass., 1771–1823, who probably received it from his father-in-law Thomas Balch, first minister of South Church in Dedham, Mass.

Essex Institute, Salem, Mass.

196

PSALMODY

The Psalms of David Imitated . . . together with Hymns and Spiritual Songs

Isaac Watts, 1674–1748

Boston, 1791.

The Congregational Library, Boston, Mass.

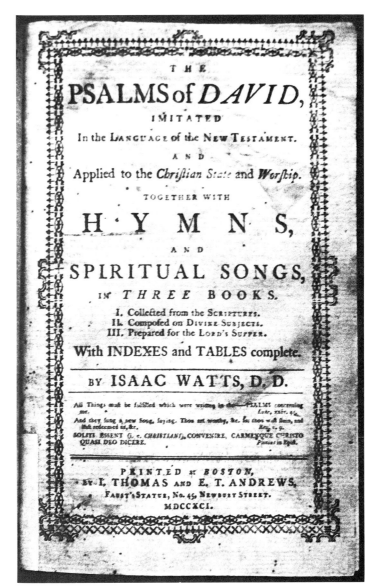

THE PSALMS of DAVID, IMITATED In the Language of the New Testament. AND Applied to the Christian State and Worship. TOGETHER WITH HYMNS, AND SPIRITUAL SONGS, IN THREE BOOKS. I. Collected from the Scriptures. II. Composed on Divine Subjects. III. Prepared for the Lord's Supper. With INDEXES and TABLES complete. BY ISAAC WATTS, D.D.

All Things must be fulfilled which were written in the PSALMS concerning me. *Luke, xxiv. 44.* And they sung a new Song, saying. Thou art worthy, &c. for thou wast slain, and hast redeemed us, &c. *Rev. v. 9.* SOLITI ESSENT (i. e. CHRISTIANI), CONVENIRE, CARMENQUE CHRISTO QUASI DEO DICERE. *Pliniws in Epift.*

PRINTED AT BOSTON, BY I. THOMAS AND E. T. ANDREWS, FAUST's STATUE, No. 45, NEWBURY STREET. MDCCXCI.

196

197

HYMNBOOK

The Massachusetts Compiler of Sacred Choral Music Together with a musical dictionary

Boston, 1795.

The Congregational Library, Boston, Mass.

Lenders to the Exhibition

American Antiquarian Society
Arlington Street Church
Barnes Museum
The Beverly Historical Society
Christ Church, Cambridge
The Congregational Library
The Connecticut Historical Society
Daughters of the American Revolution Museum
Essex Institute
First Baptist Church in America
First Parish Unitarian Church, Beverly
First and Second Church in Boston
The First Parish in Cambridge
First Congregational Church of Canterbury
First Parish Church in Dorchester
First Parish Church in Exeter
First Church of Christ Congregational,
    Farmington
First Parish Unitarian, Groton
First Church in Ipswich
First Parish, Unitarian, Kennebunk
First Parish in Lexington
First Parish Church, Ludlow
First Universalist Society in Greater Lynn
First Parish Church in Plymouth, Unitarian-
    Universalist
First Parish Church, Unitarian-Universalist,
    Portland
The First Congregational Church of Royalston
First Church in Salem, Unitarian
First Church of Christ in Sandwich
First Congregational Church of Whately
First Church in Windsor
First Congregational Church of Woodstock
Fruitlands Museum
Gore Place
Hancock Historical Society
Henry J. Harlow
Historical Society of Old Newbury
Ingalls Memorial Library
The Reverend and Mrs. Clare Milton Ingham
King's Chapel

Lempster Historical Society
Leominster Historical Society
Lyman Allyn Museum
Lynn Historical Society
Marblehead Historical Society
Massachusetts Historical Society
The Mattatuck Museum
Medfield Historical Society
Mount Holyoke College Art Museum
Museum of the Concord Antiquarian Society
Ann Parker and Avon Neal
New Haven Colony Historical Society
Northampton Historical Society
Old Gaol Museum
Old Sturbridge Village
Pilgrim Society
The Providence Athenaeum
The Rhode Island Historical Society
Rockingham Free Public Library
Rocky Hill Historical Society
St. Michael's Church Archives
Second Church in Dorchester
Shrewsbury Historical Society
The Society for the Preservation of New
    England Antiquities
Sterling Historical Commission
Tabernacle Church, United Church of Christ
    Congregational, Salem
Trinity Church in the City of Boston
The Webb-Deane-Stevens Museum
Wenham Historical Association and Museum,
    Inc.
The Westmoreland Congregational Society of the
    Park Hill Church, Inc.
Wethersfield Historical Society
The Henry Francis du Pont Winterthur Museum
Eleanor B. Wolf
Dr. and Mrs. Melvyn D. Wolf
Worcester Art Museum
Worcester Historical Museum
Yale University Art Gallery, Mabel Brady
    Garvan Collection
Private Collections

Acknowledgments

Because of the nature of its subject, this project could not have been undertaken without the assistance and voluntary contributions of numerous individuals as well as public and private institutions. First and foremost, we are indebted to Jessie and Daniel Farber of Worcester, Massachusetts, who contributed many hours and days of their own time photographing the objects. At the same time, we are also indebted to the efforts of James L. and Donna-Belle Garvin of the New Hampshire Historical Society for their sympathetic encouragement and their diligent research in New Hampshire; Robert L. Trent of the Museum of Fine Arts, Boston, for providing leads to objects in Connecticut and for his constructive criticism of the exhibition selection; Arlene M. Palmer of The Henry Francis du Pont Winterthur Museum, Delaware, for her assistance in evaluating glass and ceramic objects; John Carl Thomas of Hanover, Connecticut, for his assistance in making the pewter selection; Thompson R. Harlow of the Connecticut Historical Society for lending his support at an early stage of the search; Bettina A. Norton of the Essex Institute, Salem, and Trinity Church in the City of Boston, for her energetic and dedicated search of eastern Massachusetts; and Henry J. Harlow of Shrewsbury, Massachusetts, for his advice and the generous use of his private collection.

The interest and support of the following individuals also contributed to the success of this project: the Reverend James Allen, First Parish Church in Dorchester, Mass.; Oliver M. Ames, First and Second Church in Boston, Mass.; C. Douglass Alves, Wethersfield Historical Society, Wethersfield, Conn.; the Reverend John J. Adams and Donald S. Robie, First Parish Church in Exeter, N. H.; E. Elliott Allis, Whately, Mass.; Richard Ayer, Barbara A. R. Clinton, Alan Grimard, Susan Soule, Ernest A. Sweet, Jr., Melvin E. Watts, and Kimon S. Zachos, The Currier Gallery of Art, Manchester, N. H.; William O. Blaney, Wellesley, Mass.; William Butler, Bristol, R. I.; M. Wyllis Bibbins, Christ Church, Cambridge, Mass.; Thom W. Blair, Trinity Church in the City of Boston, Mass.; Horace L. Bachelder, First Parish Church in Plymouth, Unitarian-Universalist, Plymouth, Mass.; William Hammond Bowden, Marblehead Historical Society, Marblehead, Mass.; Mrs. Paul Becker and Carol Hagglund, First Baptist Church in America, Providence, R. I.; the Reverend James A. Barclay, First Congregational Church in Hampton, N. H.; the Reverend James K. Brown, First Congregational Church of Canterbury, Conn.; Georgia B. Bumgardner and Marcus McCorison, American Antiquarian Society, Worcester, Mass.; Fred W. Bardwell, Clerk, First Congregational Church of Whately, Mass.; Thomas G. Brennan, Albert T. Klyberg, and Ann LeVeque, The Rhode Island Historical Society, Providence, R. I.; William L. Bauhan, Dublin, N. H.; Abbott L. Cummings, Frederic C. Detwiller, Richard C. Nylander, and Judith E. Selwyn, The Society for the Preservation of New England Antiquities, Boston, Mass.; Peter Copelas and the Reverend Clifford Tobin, Tabernacle Church, United Church of Christ Congregational, Salem, Mass.; Michael Brown and Jonathan Fairbanks, Museum of Fine Arts, Boston, Mass.; Michael L. Cornog and Helmuth W. Joel, Dublin School, Dublin, N. H.; Arline R. Davis and Mr. and Mrs. Francis H. Duehay, The First Parish in Cambridge, Mass.; Edith Decker, Hancock Historical Society, Hancock, N. H.; the Reverend Robert F. Dobson and James C. Lahar, First Church in Ipswich, Mass.; Arthur Deming and the Reverend Harland Lewis, First Church of Christ Congregational, Farmington, Conn.; the Reverend Jon W. Day, First Church in Windsor, Conn.; David W. Dangremond, The Webb-Deane-Stevens Museum, Wethersfield, Conn.; Mrs. Seymour Dimaré and Caroline Stride, Museum of the Concord Antiquarian Society, Concord, Mass.; Ruth Ekberg and Barbara T. Reynolds, The Westmoreland Congregational Society of the Park Hill Church, Inc., Westmoreland, N. H.; Barry W. Eager, Berlin Historical Commission and The First Congregational Church in Berlin, Mass.; Robert Eggleston and Floyd Shumway, New Haven Colony Historical Society, New Haven, Conn.; Susan M. Eastwood and Faith Magoun, Lynn Historical Society, Lynn, Mass.; Mrs. C. E. Fraser and Betty Todd, Rindge Historical Society, Rindge, N. H.; Donald R. Friary, Historic Deerfield, Inc., Deerfield, Mass.; Joan W. Friedland, Connecticut Historical Society, Hartford, Conn.; Anne Farnam and Robinson Murray, Essex Institute, Salem, Mass.; Mr. and Mrs. Dean A. Fales, Jr., Kennebunkport, Maine; Webster Goodwin, Warwick, R. I.; Susan Grasson, First Parish Unitarian Church, Beverly, Mass.; Marian K. Greeley, First Parish in Lexington, Mass.; Jessica Goss, Paul K. Richard, and William D. Wallace, Worcester Historical Museum, Worcester, Mass.; the Reverend Richard S. Hasty, First Parish Church, Unitarian-Universalist, Portland, Maine; Russell K. Hawkins, Berlin, Mass.; Charles Hammond, Gore Place, Waltham, Mass.; David D. Hall, Boston University, Boston, Mass.; the Reverend James S. Harrison, First Congregational Church of Woodstock, Conn.; Ruth Hopfmann, Sterling Historical Commission, Sterling, Mass.; Robert L. Howie, Jr., St. Michael's Church Archives, Marblehead, Mass.; Ev-

174

elyn B. Hachey, Leominster Historical Society, Leominster, Mass.; Henry C. Horner, Worcester, Mass.; Paul A. Hurd, Medfield Historical Society, Medfield, Mass.; Mrs. Elwood Hoxie and Mary L. Niles, Old Ship Church, Hingham, Mass.; Mary S. Hafer and Mrs. A. H. Webber, Jr., The Beverly Historical Society, Beverly, Mass.; Stephen B. Jareckie, Worcester Art Museum, Worcester, Mass.; the Reverend Frank T. Jensen, Second Church in Dorchester, Mass.; Betty Joyce, Kennebunk, Maine; the Reverend and Mrs. Clare Milton Ingham, Danbury, Conn.; John T. Kirk, Boston, Mass.; Patricia E. Kane and Gerald Ward, Yale University Art Gallery, New Haven, Conn.; Mr. and Mrs. Bertram K. Little, Brookline, Mass.; Russell A. Lovell, Jr., Sandwich Archives and Historical Center, Sandwich, Mass.; Wilhelmina Lunt, Historical Society of Old Newbury, Newbury, Mass.; Ina Mansur, Bedford, Mass.; Rose Marie Mitten and Marcia Moss, Concord Free Public Library, Concord, Mass.; Dike Mason, First Church in Salem, Unitarian, Salem, Mass.; Dorothy Mayo, Bolton Historical Society, Bolton, Mass.; Nancy Merrill, Exeter Historical Society, Exeter, N. H.; Edgar deN. Mayhew, Lyman Allyn Museum, New London, Conn.; Herbert L. McChesney, First Parish Church in Ludlow, Mass.; Jeanne M. Mills and Laurence R. Pizer, Pilgrim Society, Plymouth, Mass.; Ann Parker and Avon Neal, North Brookfield, Mass.; Thomas W. Parker, The Bostonian Society, Boston, Mass.; John F. Page, New Hampshire Historical Society, Concord, N. H.; Eldridge H. Pendleton, Old Gaol Museum, York, Maine; David R. Proper, Pocumtuck Valley Memorial Association Library, Deerfield, Mass.; the Reverend Peter T. Richardson, First Parish Unitarian, Kennebunk, Maine; Peter J. Revill, Rocky Hill Historical Society, Rocky Hill, Conn.; Richard S. Reed, Fruitlands Museum, Harvard, Mass.; Harrison Ripley, First Parish Unitarian, Groton, Mass.; Gladys M. Ring, Congregational Church of Acworth, N. H.; Carol Smith, Arlington Street Church, Boston, Mass.; Karol A. Schmiegal and James Morton Smith, The Henry Francis du Pont Winterthur Museum, Winterthur, Del.; Gail Seybold, Old South Church, Boston, Mass.; Ann Smith, The Mattatuck Museum, Waterbury, Conn.; Thatcher Spencer, King's Chapel, Boston, Mass.; Cynthia Saccoccia, The Providence Athenaeum, Providence, R. I.; Louise Stevenson, Boston University, Boston, Mass.; Robert Blair St. George, Philadelphia, Pa.; Susan C. Tucker, Concord, Mass.; Eleanor E. Thompson, Wenham Historical Association and Museum, Inc., Wenham, Mass.; Jean Taylor-Frederico, Daughters of the American Revolution Museum, Washington, D. C.; Muriel Thomas, Rockingham Free Public Library, Bellows Falls, Vt.; Everett Thurber,

Lempster, N. H.; Louis L. Tucker, John D. Cushman, and Ross Urquhart, Massachusetts Historical Society, Boston, Mass.; Harold F. Worthley, The Congregational Library, Boston, Mass.; Dr. Phillip Williams, First Universalist Society in Greater Lynn, Swampscott, Mass.; Milton J. Wooding, Barnes Museum, Southington, Conn.; the Reverend James Willis, The First Congregational Church of Royalston, Mass.; Ruth E. Wilbur, Northampton Historical Society, Northampton, Mass.; Wendy M. Watson, Mt. Holyoke College Art Museum, South Hadley, Mass.; William L. Warren, Fitzwilliam, N. H.; Eleanor B. Wolf, Wethersfield, Conn.; Dr. and Mrs. Melvyn D. Wolf, Flint, Mich.; Lawrence J. Yerdon, Quincy Historical Society, Quincy, Mass.; and Florence C. Young, Woodstock, Conn.

Finally, this project would have been impossible without the unflagging support of Jane Montague Benes, whose efforts kept the project on an even course and saw it through to its successful conclusion.

Peter Benes
Philip D. Zimmerman

Photo Credits

(numbers refer to catalogue entry)

Daniel Farber: 1, 2, 5–8, 13, 16–19, 22–24, 26–37, 44–51, 54, 55, 58, 64, 66–71, 73–75, 77–79, 81, 82, 87–89, 91–93, 101, 102, 104–106, 109, 114–116, 118, 120–123, 128, 129, 131, 132, 137, 157, 158, 173, 174, 176, 180, 181, 183–185, 187, 191

Philip D. Zimmerman: 4, 12, 25, 53, 95, 96, 97, 103, 107, 110, 113, 119, 125, 133, 134, 136, 141, 142, 144–149, 151, 153, 154, 156, 162, 164–172, 175, 176, 179

Peter Benes: 38, 43, 57, 59, 61, 62, 117, 130, 178, 188, 196

Bill Finney, courtesy of New Hampshire Historical Society: 11, 14, 135, 159, 161, 189, 190, 192

Cushing Photography: 10, 15, 83, 182

J. David Bohl, The Society for the Preservation of New England Antiquities: 76, 86, 90, 98

Richard Merrill, Photographer: 3

Courtesy of The Pilgrim Society: 9

Courtesy of Essex Institute, Salem: 20

Courtesy of John Carter Brown Library, Brown University: 21

Courtesy of Lyman Allyn Museum: 39

Courtesy of American Antiquarian Society: 40

Courtesy of The Henry Francis du Pont Winterthur Museum: 41, 143

Helga Photo Studio: 42

Courtesy of Worcester Historical Museum: 52

Courtesy of The Sandwich Historical Society: 56

Courtesy of The Northampton Historical Society: 65

Courtesy of The Ipswich Historical Society: 74 (sounding board)

Herbert McChesney: 84

Courtesy of the Marblehead Historical Society: 85

Courtesy of the First Congregational Church, Woodstock, Conn.: 111

Courtesy of Old Sturbridge Village: 112

Courtesy of the Worcester Art Museum: 127

Courtesy of the Museum of Fine Arts, Boston: 138, 139, 140

Courtesy of the Yale University Art Gallery: 150

Joseph Kitrosser, Lexington, Mass.: 152

Courtesy of the Mattatuck Museum: 155

Courtesy of the Connecticut Historical Society: 160

Courtesy of Old Gaol Museum, York, Maine: 175

Courtesy of Henry J. Harlow: 177

Herbert P. Vose: 186

Mark Sexton: 193

DATE DUE

DEMCO, INC. 38-2931